M000045189

THE OTHER WOMAN

Bootie,

Let's show the
world who God
is! BTM! :)

ZAPA

:)

Tunette Powell

Copyright ©2012 Tunette Powell

All rights reserved. No part of this book may
be reproduced or transmitted in any form or by
any means, electronic or mechanical, including
photocopying, recording, or by any information
storage and retrieval system, without permission in
writing from publisher.

Published by WriteLife, LLC
2323 S. 171 St.
Suite 202
Omaha, NE 68130
www.writelife.com

Printed in the United States of America

ISBN 978 1 60808 074 8

First Edition

DEDICATION

To my father,

As the African Proverb teaches us, "When there is no enemy within, the enemies outside cannot hurt you."

We have harbored these stories for so many years because we were hurt, embarrassed and ashamed of them. But if we want to lead people off the porch and if we want to encourage people to recycle the human life, we must tell our story.

Though painful, I pray that our story helps someone else. Most importantly, I hope it heals us.

Love,
Nette

CONTENTS

TRACK 1

Hi, my name is Tunette and my father is a drug addict.

There, I said it.

For a long time, I pretended as if my father's addiction didn't affect me. Sure, I hated his addiction. Growing up, I spent so many nights crying and begging God to deliver my father. But I never prayed for myself. I just pushed my feelings aside because I didn't want to be guilty of violating my father's golden rule.

"I before E, Nette," my father used to say. "Intellect before emotion."

Somewhere along the way, I became so focused on not breaking that rule that I was blind to what was happening to me. It had been years since he first said those words. But it didn't matter. My father's words never expired. Whenever something was wrong, memories of old prison letters haunted my thoughts and reminded me that emotions have no place on a sleeve.

Then a few years ago, I lost control of my emotions for the first time. My father was in prison. I was twenty one. And by that time, writing and receiving letters from my father was old. I dedicated most of my childhood to licking envelopes, pressing stamps and reading my father's cursive handwriting on white tablet paper. And even though at a young age I vowed to never give up on my father, I had to admit it was getting harder to keep that promise.

As a child, wounds healed days after they appeared. But as an adult, not even bandages could hide my scars. My heart was a bunch of pieces with no instruction manual. I tried to repair myself through relationships. I dated way too many boys and carelessly flirted with way too many girls. Even as young as five-years-old, I sought that attention. While most girls were grossed out by boys in elementary, I skipped right past that "boys have cooties" stage.

There was a hunger in me that craved for attention and approval.

And I fed it.

My freshman year of high school was tarnished by my obsession with attention. That year, I went to an all-black high school and starred on the freshman girls' basketball team. And even though I was closer to Gary Coleman's height than Lisa Leslie's, I thought I would go on to play in the WNBA. After practice, I would join in with my teammates as we pretended to be gay. We wrote and exchanged inappropriate letters and pretended to be in intimate relationships with each other. Now that I'm ten years removed from that freshman year, it sounds silly. But at fourteen, I was looking for anything to distract me; anything to replace the emptiness I felt. I wasn't attracted to girls.

I was attracted to attention.

It was the only way I knew how to cope with my father's absence. As I recklessly tried to fill that void, I broke so many hearts. Brendon was one of those broken hearts.

"I love you," I randomly proclaimed one day.

"I love you, too," Brendon confessed.

I didn't love Brendon. I just wanted him to love me. Brendon wasn't the first boy I'd done that to, and surely not the last. I was a blank sheet waiting to be called music. And I didn't care how the notes got on the page. I thought to myself that as long as I wasn't on the broken end of the equation, it didn't matter. I knew one thing – I would never let another person walk out on me the way my father did. No man would ever two-time me the way my father did our family with drugs.

But there I was; sitting in the passenger's seat of Maurice's black Honda Accord with my hands over my face because I was too shy to look him in his eyes. He was in the driver's seat reciting Tupac lyrics, and trying to convince me that Jay-Z was not the best rapper alive. In between Maurice rapping along to Tupac's "Blasphemy", we talked politics, religion and eventually love. Normally by the time we got to love, his phone rang.

It was her.

I was just his side chick. I knew that from the beginning. Initially, I only flirted with Maurice to see if he would flirt back. But then I became infatuated with his style – his intellect, his taste in food, music, sports, and so many other things.

Then I fell in love.

Love was never a part of the plan. I knew it would be difficult to remain in control if my emotions got involved. But before I could pull my heart back in, it had already run away. And his girlfriend, well, she was only a technicality. Or at least that's what I told myself.

"Think of us as a marathon and not a sprint," I remember him saying.

And for a while, I did that.

I got used to the frequent text messages and phone calls while he was at work and the silence in the evenings when he was at home. This unhealthy co-relationship almost lasted an entire year. Until one day, it all came falling down.

It was Memorial Day. Maurice called and asked if he could come over after he got off work, and I said yes. In between his phone call and his arrival, for the first time, I sat on my couch and really thought things out. I was in love with a man who was living with another woman. And it didn't bother me. As tears fell down my eyes, I ran into the restroom, looked myself in the mirror and hated the woman I saw.

I cried out to God, but this time I asked him to deliver me. When Maurice got to my apartment, we argued. He left; I closed the door behind him, and pressed my back against the door as I cried. That night I rushed out of my apartment and sank into the driver's seat of my 2002 peanut-butter-colored Saturn. I locked the car doors, positioned my head on the steering wheel and cried like a baby. Then I reached into my backseat, grabbed a pen and notepad, and started to write. I didn't write a letter to my father, nor was it a letter to Maurice.

I wrote to myself.

I ignored my father's advice and put my emotions out there. I couldn't hide my feelings in men anymore. I needed something else. I needed something stronger. With an instrumental beat in my head, I started writing a rap.

It's gotta be a nightmare; it's gotta be a dream, I started out.

And it was a nightmare. I didn't know who I'd become. But instead of the next line being about me, it was about my father.

Envisioning a father transform into fiend.

I blacked out.

When I came back to, the rap was written.

It's gotta be a nightmare, it's gotta be a dream,
Envisioning a father transform into a fiend,
Rapes his family of their goods and flirts with the world,
Traded in his baby girl for that white girl,
Always told her that he loved her most,
'My daddy loves me,' jokingly she boasts,
But the truth backs her down; it got her in the post,
Running to the arms of the past, but he's a ghost,
And how is she supposed to conquer and be strong,
When the one man that she loves has done her wrong,
Promising to stop and be a better father,
Yet tip-toeing out to pawn the VCR,
Out three days, that's 72 hours,

Crazy to see how much food he devours,
Gulping down vinegar to clean out his system,
She runs to the door, I guess she missed him.

When I looked back over the rap, each bar and line told a story of their own. All of the secrets I'd hidden, both my father's and my own, trickled through that verse. Bar after bar, I started reliving past hurts. And for the first time, it seemed okay to show my emotions. I knew that the next day I'd have to go back to being whatever my father needed me to be.

But for the night, I needed to run away.

TRACK 2

The floors were bare.

The walls were white.

The furniture was dingy.

People loped in and out of the kitchen like New Yorkers on a subway at morning rush hour. One after another, they stood near the lit stove, rubbing their hands together to keep warm.

There was a young girl, wearing a halter top and tight-fitted blue jeans, hovering over the stove top amongst the cluster, holding something in her hand.

She was biracial – probably white and black – with hair that flowed like ocean waves. The stains in her once-white halter top and blue jeans hinted at the number of days since she last showered. But there was something about her eyes; there was innocence in them.

"What's your name?" my father asked her.

"Becky," she said in a low, soft tone.

"What are you doing here?"

Becky was a seventeen-year-old runaway who shuffled in and out of foster homes and orphanages. Becky looked like she should have been a news anchor or talk show host. But it was hard to survive on the streets sober, so she had to do what she had to do.

"You smoke?" my father asked as he looked down at the crack pipe in her hand.

He already knew the answer.

People only gathered at Kitty's apartment for two reasons – to smoke crack or to sell it.

And Becky wasn't a dope dealer.

* * *

My father was married to my mother at the time, but he couldn't take his eyes off of her. Becky was beautiful. She wasn't a typical female dope head – women so strung out that their mouths twitched profusely and uncontrollably. Women like that were a dime a dozen at Kitty's apartment. But there were very few like Becky.

Becky didn't know Kitty, but she had heard that his place was a safe haven for addicts. Everybody had heard of Kitty – all the neighborhood folks, cops, dealers and fiends. But the cops had no clue that Kitty was running a crack house. Most people felt sorry for him because he didn't have legs. And he preyed on people's sympathy.

He sat on street corners, not too far from his house, in a wheelchair, beating his hands against bongo drums. Kitty treated that street corner as though it was a stage. The drivers who got caught at the red light were his audience. As they watched, they rolled their windows down and threw money at him. When Kitty wasn't on that corner, he was securing his apartment. Even though it was a crack house, Kitty ran a tight ship. He was selective with whom he let deal at his house.

My father sold crack at Kitty's house. Kitty and my dad weren't the coolest cats on the block, but they had an understanding. My father wasn't one of those loud-suit-gold-chain-wearing wannabes. He was always low-key. And Kitty trusted him.

My father got his work from Cubans. They had the purest cocaine in the city. It wasn't hard to tell the difference in the quality between theirs and someone else's in your neighborhood. My father was working for a Cuban named Papa. Just months before my father started selling crack; President Fidel Castro shipped a boatload of refugees to South Florida to rid Cuba of some of its criminals. Papa was one of those refugees. He was a black Cuban – about the same color as a Snickers bar.

My father was in the Denver Heights when he first heard of Papa. The Denver Heights was nothing more than project housing for Mexicans. And most of them got high. My father used to hang out in the Denver Heights looking for people who would let him smoke weed and snort a line of cocaine at their house. This Mexican lady and her husband used to let him smoke at their apartment for five dollars. They were heroin addicts.

My father shot up heroin once or twice with the couple, but he didn't like it. Heroin made him feel depressed and sluggish. He mostly just smoked marijuana blunts laced with cocaine. And he sold a little cocaine on the side, too, but he didn't have a good connect.

The heroin addicts knew my father was looking

to score some cocaine, so they introduced him to another Mexican couple that lived on Grayson Street, just outside downtown. They told my father that the Cubans were regulars at a nearby club, and they were looking for local drug dealers; ones that were loyal and had a steady clientele.

My father walked to the club alone.

He dressed down – not too clean, but not too shabby. And he used a fake name. Papa sat in the back of the club. He was short and had a thick beard. He looked black.

"You know girls?" Papa asked.

By girls, he meant black women. Cubans loved black women. My father told him he would throw a couple of girls his way. Papa dug that. Papa didn't speak too much English, and the English he did speak was broken. But he knew enough to get at a girl and to gauge a drug dealer's loyalty.

That same night Papa and my father became business partners. My father always told me that a deal with the Cubans was like a deal with the devil. They were the most dangerous people my father ever encountered. They didn't make idle threats. And they were real stupid when they got mad.

But it was worth it.

The cocaine Papa had was so pure that whenever my father cooked the cocaine to crack, he could see oil inside of it. The oil meant it was potent. And if you smoked cocaine that was potent, it left a lasting impression – almost like a fingerprint on glass.

My father was a small-time dealer, mostly selling

to people he knew. He purchased fifty packs for fifty dollars each. From there, he broke it down and sold it as five twenty rocks. Each fifty pack turned over a fifty-dollar profit.

He sold most of his dope at Kitty's house; mostly to men customers because women were always broke at crack houses. They knew they could seduce a dealer into giving them drugs in exchange for sex.

Becky didn't have any money.

"What you looking for?" my father asked.

Becky didn't answer. Instead, she held up the crack pipe she had been holding.

"How much you got?" my father asked.

My father knew Becky didn't have any money. She had been standing in the kitchen trying to get a hit from another guy's pipe as he lit it at the kitchen stove. She put her head down and walked to the back of Kitty's apartment. There were two bedrooms in the back of Kitty's apartment.

The bedroom in the back, where Becky was headed, didn't have anything in it except for a mattress – no box spring, no comforter. Roaches crept up the sides of the mattress. And junkies sat, with their eyes closed, alongside the walls of the bedroom. Becky walked toward the mattress.

My father followed her.

"Do you smoke?" she asked my father.

"A little bit," he said. "I smoke it like a cigarette."

"You ever smoked it with a pipe?"

"Naw...never."

The room was silent. The outside streetlight was

the room's only source of light, and it flickered off. My father and Becky lay next to each other on top of the mattress. My father grabbed Becky's hand and put it in his pants. Becky did the rest. She and my father lay in bed all night, taking turns performing sexual acts. And in between, Becky got high off nickel rocks.

"Try it," she told him.

Before he could respond, Becky put the pipe to his mouth and lit it. For a split second, his entire body felt as though it had ejaculated. But the high left so quickly. He wanted to feel it again. So he and Becky hit a dime rock.

And then another.

"I can't smoke all this up," my father told Becky. "I gotta sell this."

By sun up, he had smoked the crack he was supposed to sell. It was like a song stuck in his head. Even when he tried to forget the lyrics, he couldn't. Becky was gone the next morning. She got her high, so she was good. My father went back home.

"I'm in a little bit of trouble," my father told my mother. "I need some money."

"What happened?"

"Man, I didn't make as much money as I thought I would out there last night."

My mother handed him all the cash she had in her purse. She didn't like my father selling drugs, but the extra money fed her love for designer clothing and mink coats.

My father left and went looking for Papa. Papa was staying at a motel, but he didn't want to draw too much attention. Papa was afraid that cars pulling up and out of the motel would alert the cops. So my father had to walk to the motel if he wanted to meet with him. My father walked eight miles to meet with Papa. When he got there, Papa knew something was different. It wasn't hard to spot a junkie. But all Papa cared about was his profit. My father bought a fifty pack of cocaine and left. He tried to sell it at Kitty's house.

But he couldn't.

My father scampered into Kitty's kitchen amongst the cluster and lit his pipe from the kitchen stove.

TRACK 3

I have always wondered if my older brother Brushaud ever believed in Santa Claus or if my father robbed him of that childhood privilege. It was a long time ago, but none of us could forget it. I was only eleven-months-old, but I could tell it as if I was much older.

Brushaud was just seven, but he was old enough to understand a lot more than most adults gave him credit for. He was old enough to notice my father taking off with my mother's last few dollars and our only source of transportation. And he was old enough to know when my mother dressed up a situation.

Brushaud knew we weren't riding the bus to take the scenic route, nor were we catching a ride with one of my mother's coworkers because they wanted to see us. And even though he was mature for his age, he was still just a kid. That Christmas, Brushaud told my mother he wanted a game of Jacks, marbles, and some little green army men. But he didn't expect to get it. His holiday spirit was dwarfed by his ghost of Christmas past.

Just three years before on the same day, my father

dropped my mother and Brushaud off at a Christmas Eve party at my mother's job. I wasn't born yet. Brushaud was four-years-old and just old enough to understand what Christmas was. My mother thought that seeing Santa Claus at the party would ignite a spark of happiness in Brushaud. Every Christmas leading up to that one had been a humbling one. My mother only made $2.95 an hour and my father's income was sporadic. He worked odd jobs when he could and sold drugs on the side.

But my parents struggled.

When the party ended, my mother and an overjoyed Brushaud stood outside waiting for my father. He promised to be back by the time the party ended.

"Brushaud, you want to catch the bus home?" my mother asked thirty minutes later.

Brushaud nodded and followed my mother to the nearest bus stop.

"This is going to be fun," my mother said.

The next morning, my mother watched Brushaud open the few gifts they could afford to get him. A few hours later, my father trotted in.

"I need some money," he told my mother after selling her a million lies about where he'd been the night before.

"For what?"

"I didn't sell as much as I was supposed to for these guys, and I need to pay them."

My mother gave him all the money she had in her purse. My father stormed out with no mention of Christmas. When he showed up a few days later, my mother knew he was no longer just selling drugs; he was using them.

Three years later, my father was better. But Brushaud's memory was still bitter. But he put up a good front for my mother. The Christmas season was her favorite time of the year. Just as she had the past two years, my mother was asked to host a Christmas Eve party at our apartment. We lived in a two-bedroom apartment on the southeast side of San Antonio. It wasn't the projects, but it wasn't luxurious either. We lived amongst people where twenty-five dollars and a cheap case of beer could solve any dispute. But my mother knew how to fancy it up. She always decorated our apartment with Christmas lights and a real Christmas tree. She never put gifts under the tree because she wanted us to believe in Santa Claus.

That Christmas Eve morning, she and my father went Christmas shopping. I was barely walking and the most I could say were simple two-letter syllables, so they didn't buy me very many gifts. But my parents went all out for Brushaud. My mother saved up as much money as she could to guarantee Brushaud his first real Christmas. My parents stuffed the trunk of our car with so many toys and clothes that my father had to push down on the items just to close the trunk.

Over that three-year course, my father made a lot of mistakes. But he had been clean for more than a month. He seemed better. Unlike past holidays, my father was excited. He was proud to be playing Santa to our imaginations.

After a morning and afternoon of shopping, my

parents picked us up from my grandma's house and we headed home. My mother wanted to make it home in time to clean up and prepare dinner for the party. As always, enchiladas with beans and rice were on the menu. It was a Christmas Eve staple in our family.

As my mother stood in the kitchen rolling enchiladas, the phone rang.

"Hey Tulane," my Aunt Tandy said on the other line. "Junior went hunting, so I'm gonna need a ride."

"Okay," my mother told her. "Bruce will be by there to pick you up."

Tandy only lived about fifteen minutes away, so she knew it wouldn't take my father any longer than thirty or forty minutes to return. That was enough time for her to finish rolling the enchiladas and grating the cheese. After she put the enchiladas in the oven, she put a Motown Christmas cassette tape in the stereo. Brushaud and I sat around the living room, listening to my mother sing as though she was on stage performing.

My mother always said my love for music was passed down to me just like the structure of my face and the curls in my hair. My mother was so caught up in the moment that she didn't realize an hour had passed.

And then the phone rang.

"Hey Tulane," my Aunt Tandy said as my mother answered the phone. "What time was Bruce coming?"

"He should be there any minute," my mother said as she looked over at the clock.

My mother waited another hour before calling Tandy back.

"I don't think he's going to come," my mother told her.

Tandy got a ride with my granny. And my mother carried on as though nothing was wrong. The party was set to start at seven o'clock, but everyone made it around eight. My family was never on time. The ongoing joke was that we would all be late to our own funerals.

My grandparents, aunts, uncles, and cousins arrived. Everybody seemed a little worried about my mother. But she kept it together. She smiled and enjoyed herself as though my father was standing next to her. The kids played. The adults laughed, talked, and sang Christmas carols and old school music. My mother and all five of her sisters went back and forth singing Natalie Cole's 1975 classic hit, "This Will Be".

All the women in my family could sing except for me. And even though I couldn't, I still had a knack for music. As I got older, I went from embarrassing myself as I tried to hold a note, to writing raps on notepads.

Just before the party ended, my father's mother called.

"Levester just called and said he saw Bruce out in the Sutton Homes selling toys out the trunk of his car," my grandma told my mother.

When my mother got out of the car earlier she had me on one hip and groceries on the other. She didn't think about the gifts in the trunk.

"Do you have any toys at the house?" my grandma asked.

"Just one baby doll," my mother replied.

"You want me to bring some of the toys I have?"

My mother declined her offer. My grandma never drove at night. And there was no way my mother was going to send my grandma out in the middle of the night.

"No," my mother said. "We'll be all right."

After my mother got off the phone, she kissed and hugged everybody as they headed out the door. Then my mother tided up and put me and Brushaud to bed. She never said anything to Brushaud.

The next morning, Brushaud woke up first and ran into the living room to see what Santa had brought us. But when he got into the living room, there was only one gift under the tree. It was a baby doll.

"You don't have no gifts under the tree because they were in the trunk of the car and your daddy..." my mother said as she paused mid-sentence.

She didn't know what to say. Brushaud's eyes glared with a kid-like innocence yet with so much wisdom. My mother didn't want to tell Brushaud the truth, but he knew it already.

"I know Daddy probably took them," Brushaud said.

"Yea... but you'll have gifts at Grandma's house."

"I know," Brushaud said. "As long as Tunette's happy, I'm okay."

Brushaud was only seven-years-old, but he kept it together. He sat near the Christmas tree, smiling as I opened the only present my father didn't get the chance to sell. As I tore open the baby doll packaging, Brushaud clapped and cheered me on. He should've been sad, but the expectations were already set. He would've been surprised if things had gone right.

My mother clapped and cheered, too. If she was hurt, she never let us see her pain. After I opened my gift, she threw the box away and got us ready to go to my grandma's.

"Brushaud, you're going to have a lot of presents at grandma's house," my mom told him.

He looked up at her and smiled. My mother got us dressed and called my grandma's house so that somebody could give us a ride.

As promised, Brushaud had a lot of gifts under my grandma's tree. My mother had some, too. As Christmas faded into three days later, my father finally came home.

"You really messed up this time," my mother told him. "You know... that was the saddest thing for Brushaud to wake up on Christmas and not have any gifts."

"I'm sorry," my father pleaded. "I'm gone make up for it."

My father really was sorry. He wasn't a horrible person; he was an addict. His addiction serenaded him whenever he felt lonely, bored or too excited. When he left the house that night to pick up Tandy, my father was more excited than he'd ever been on a holiday. That burst of excitement was too much. My mother understood that. And even though this wasn't his first Christmas Eve breakdown, my mother gave in to my father's plea as if she'd never heard it before.

But not Brushaud; to him, it was all a broken record.

TRACK 4

I was conceived on the same day my Uncle Geanie, my father's brother, buried his one-year-old son. The details of his death are still sketchy, but he died at a daycare. The death was enough of a tragedy for my father to be temporarily released from the Patrician Movement, a drug treatment center on the South Side of San Antonio.

My parents had been married for five years, and although two of those years were overshadowed by drug dealing and drug abuse, my mother still held out hope for my father.

After the funeral, my mother and father went to my Aunt Linda's house. Linda was my father's oldest sister. She still lived in the Sutton Homes – the projects my father and his five siblings grew up in.

My mother and Brushaud, who was five years old, moved in with my Aunt Linda around the same time my father entered rehab.

My mother didn't have a choice.

Even though she still worked as a manager at the beverage company, my mother's credit was awful and her savings account was nonexistent.

But on that day, none of that mattered.

I guess you could say my parents were prisoners of the moment. In the same bedroom my father once shared with his older brothers, he told my mother he wanted another child.

She never objected.

* * *

"Tunette needs some milk," my mother said to my father in a whisper.

Like most mothers after a full day with an eights month old, my mother was worn out. My father knew that.

"I'll go get her some," he replied.

* * *

My father spent about ten months at the Patrician Movement. Family days at the center were on Wednesdays.

My mother never missed a Wednesday.

It was difficult for my mother in the beginning. My father resisted to the program. He wanted to continue using drugs. Every phone call my mother received was one from my father begging her to sneak weed into the rehab.

She never did.

The longer he stayed there, the easier things got. By the time he was released, he was a different man. He didn't have the same crack lust in eyes. The hunger was fulfilled by constant prayer and counseling.

He was released from the program a month before I was born.

Right around the time he got out, my mother had saved up enough money to move out of Linda's house and into an apartment on the East Side.

My father got a job as a security guard. For the first time in years, we seemed like a cookie-cutter family.

In that ninth month of my mother's pregnancy, my father did everything a father was supposed to do. He went to Lamaze classes with my mother and was in the delivery room when my mother gave birth.

My father swore I'd be a boy.

"I knew it," my father yelled out cheerfully in the delivery room. "I got another boy."

"You better open her legs," the doctor smirked.

I wasn't the boy he hoped for, but my father was proud. He chose the name Tunette. I grew to love my name mostly because of the first four letters: t-u-n-e. It always made me think of music. My mother said she could count on two fingers the number of times she'd seen my father truly happy. My birth date was one of them.

For the first time in a long time, things seemed different. My father had been out of rehab for nine months and clean the whole time. He worked the graveyard shift as a security guard, but returned back home every morning.

* * *

"She has one more bottle that she'll probably take in an hour," my mother said, "but when she wakes up in the morning, she won't have any milk left."

My father hurried to put on a T-shirt and a pair of shoes. It was just after 10 p.m. Brushaud was asleep and after that last bottle, I would be, too.

"Okay," my father said as he grabbed the car keys. "I'll be right back."

My mother handed him her last twenty dollars, and he left.

My father never returned with the formula.

As 10 p.m. faded into midnight, my mother knew she had to call somebody. My father had everything – my mother's car and her last twenty dollars.

"Bruce left to get Tunette some milk, and he never came back," my mother told my grandma.

My mother's voice sounded like a broken a record. It was the same ole tune, over and over. My father's actions no longer carried shock-value.

But everyone still pretended as though they did.

"What?" my grandma shouted out on the other end of the phone. "I can't believe he did that."

"Yea, he left with my last twenty dollars," my mother said. "Tunette has enough to make it to the next morning, but after that she is going to need some more milk."

"I'm sorry baby, I just can't believe Bruce," my grandma said. "I'll bring some formula by there in the morning."

My grandma lived on the East Side, too. It was about a five-minute drive. As promised, my grandma brought the milk the next morning.

As always, my father returned a few days later with a bunch of "I'm sorry" and "I'll make it up to you" lies.

He fell back into his regular pattern – crack binges and everything that came with it. He quit going to work. My mother fell behind on the bills and once again, we were forced to move.

My mother eventually convinced my father to go back to the Patrician Movement. It was the same old routine – family days on Wednesdays. She hauled me and Brushaud to the rehab center every week.

She never stopped believing in my father.

After watching my Uncle Geanie bury the cousin I never got to meet, my mother thought having another child would bury my father's past and mishaps. And if that wasn't enough, then she was banking on the sixty-day rehab treatment.

But it didn't take him long to find that old broken tune. He went back to drugs. He went back to stealing from us, leaving Brushaud at parks and movie theaters and dropping me off at my grandma's house while he got high. He was in love with drugs. She was his first tune; his first song.

I was just a background singer.

TRACK 5

"You can do whatever you want in here," a guy told my father.

"I'm cool, man," my father replied.

My father never smoked crack when he was in jail. He said he couldn't imagine being caged and high at the same time.

* * *

"Hold this," my father told a Mexican woman as he handed her a steel dish scrubbing pad. After twisting the scrubbing pad and stuffing it into the hallow part of a car antenna, my father used it as a makeshift screen to go over his apparatus.

On the streets, apparatus was the code word for a crack pipe.

He used alcohol bottles and aluminum foil to make an apparatus. Whenever he could afford it, he traded in the alcohol bottles and aluminum foil for three-to-four inch tubes of glass. He sat the crack rock right on top of the scrubbing pad and took a hit.

Then he passed it to the Mexican woman.

* * *

There were few prisons or jails worse than the county jail. It had an unclean smell – one of butts, musty armpits, and a wet mop. It was an institutional smell. The living arrangements were two-man cell blocks. A wooden door separated the living quarters from the day room. My father sat in his cell, contemplating his defense. He was facing five-to-ninety-nine years for a first-degree felony.

* * *

"I'm looking for a twenty-rock," a white man said as he signaled for my father to come toward his truck.

Rained poured down. My father stood on the corner of Hackberry and Commerce, still high from smoking with the Mexican woman. It was the second day into my father's involuntary fast of no food and water. He hadn't slept or put anything into his body except for crack.

My father didn't know the white men, but he wanted to get out of the rain and he wanted to get high. He got in the car with them. They pulled up at a McDonald's, not too far from the projects my father grew up in.

The projects were the easiest places to find drugs.

My father walked to the Sutton Homes. The men stayed in the truck.

"Hey, my daughter is at work and I got the place all to myself," Pimp yelled out to my father as he walked through the hallway. Pimp was an addict and a prostitute.

"You do?" my father asked. "Well, check this out...I got these white boys up at the McDonald's waiting for me..."

My father was planning to hustle the white boys – give them the dope, get them high and wanting more, and then take their money.

"I'm gone spring these punks," my father told Pimp. "You gone wait for me?"

She nodded her head yes, and my father walked back to the truck with two twenty rocks – one in his mouth and one in his pocket.

"Drive off," my father said as soon as he got in the truck.

"At least show it to me first," one white guy insisted.

* * *

My father was at the county jail for eighteen months. After months of fighting the first-degree felony, he was sentenced to fifteen years. From the county jail, my father's next stop was the Darrington Unit in Rosharon, Texas. It was right outside of Houston.

The Darrington Unit was the worse prison in the state.

The living arrangements were the same as the county jail – two-man cell blocks. But the guards were ghetto. They didn't care what the inmates did. The guards let them fight, rape other inmates, and use drugs.

It was a maximum security unit. The prison was surrounded with metal fences and barbed wire. Prison guards stood atop the unit in guard towers. But smuggling drugs at the unit was as easy as boiling water.

My father was still in transit, which meant that Darrington was only a temporary stop. He was still waiting for a long-term prison assignment. He was only allowed to shower every two-to-three days in transit. In the two weeks he spent at Darrington, he wore the same top and bottom and only changed into clean socks and underwear as often as he showered.

From Darrington, my father went to the Diagnostics Unit in Huntsville, Texas. Huntsville was the best place to be for any prisoner. It was the brain of the Texas Department of Corrections. The food was good. The prison was clean. Most importantly, the guards were nice. It didn't matter which unit it was, if it was in Huntsville then it was a good prison.

My father only spent ten days at the Diagnostics Unit before he was transferred to the Goree Unit. Goree was in Huntsville, too. At Goree, the inmates didn't live in cells; they lived in cubicles. Cubicles were partially closed rooms that were furnished with a single bunk and a desk. They were divided by four-foot walls. When my father was lying down, he couldn't see anyone else. That's what he liked most about cubicles.

In the real world, most people introduced themselves with a first and last name. But in prison, people only wanted to know where you were from. People from the same city were expected to run together. It was an unwritten rule. My father was still in transit, so Goree – like the other prisons – was supposed to be a temporary stop.

"Sir, I just want to go to a prison where I don't have to worry about nobody trying to hurt me and me trying to hurt nobody," my father told a man who was processing his paperwork.

"Well, what prison is that?"

"This one.... I want to stay at Goree."

A prison guard who knew my father as a kid vouched for my father and the board agreed to let him stay at Goree. At Goree, every inmate was assigned to a job. My father worked the graveyard shift as a janitor. As a janitor, my father could eat whatever he wanted, but the hours were poor and the work was hard.

My father wasn't a janitor for very long.

"Where they got you working at?" one of the head prison guards asked my father.

"Man, I'm working nights as a janitor."

"Man, I want you somewhere else," the guard said. "I want you in A1-south."

A few weeks later, my father was transferred to A1-south. It was transit lock-up. He worked days and evenings, but never nights. He worked as an overseer of the transit inmates. He made sure people took showers and got the clothes they needed. He also made sure everyone had a chance to go to the commissary.

* * *

As my father pulled the twenty-rock out of his pocket, the white men in the truck pulled guns on him.

"You're under arrest," one of the men yelled as he pulled out a pair of handcuffs.

"You got me," my father said as he put his hands behind his back.

Immediately, a police car pulled up behind the truck. My father was arrested for possession of a controlled substance with the intent to distribute. The officers hauled him to the county jail. My father was only charged with possession of a twenty-rock. He went to jail with the other twenty-rock still in his mouth.

No one ever searched his mouth.

* * *

My father didn't like thinking too much about the things that landed him in Huntsville. It was easy for a person to go crazy in prison.

He knew that.

He was focused on getting out. The only downside to prison life in Huntsville was making parole. Everything was by the book, which also meant that an inmate couldn't make parole without attending some sort of school. My father chose to go to school for air condition and refrigeration. He caught on quickly, and he was ready to showcase his skills to the outside world.

Three years into his sentence at Goree, he made parole. He promised himself he wasn't going to use anymore. But with a criminal record and a prison state of mind, he didn't have a plan of action. Before he knew it, that itch was back. And he scratched it.

"You remember Pimp," another user asked my father.

"Yea man, I was about to hit that the night I got arrested," my father replied.

"She died."

"What?" my father said in disbelief. "How did she die?"

"AIDS…"

TRACK 6

The six years – including kindergarten – that I spent in elementary school were the best and worst of times. I kissed my first boy, learned to play my first instrument, and wrote my first rap. It was an eight-bar verse about how big and bad my alter ego was. Her name was Lady T.

Elementary school was also where I first learned that my father was a crack head.

"Shut up, ugly," I shouted at a boy in my third-grade class during recess.

"You shut up, you ugly crack head," he yelled back.

"Yo' mama's a crack head," I charged back even louder.

"Yo' Daddy!"

We always called each other crack heads and other inappropriate names. It never bothered me to hear that someone thought I was ugly or that my mother was a crack head because I knew it wasn't true. It didn't hurt until I heard a kid say my father was a crack head. I was no fool; I knew my father was addicted to drugs. I also knew that the drug was crack cocaine. And even so, I never thought of him as a crack head.

But that's exactly what he was.

Hearing someone call my father a crack head was a lot like hearing the word nigga. It was cool if I heard it in a hip-hop verse, but it was intolerable if it came out of a white person's mouth. That kid wasn't white and he didn't call me a nigga, but it felt that way.

It hurt the same.

What hurt more than the words from the lips of an eight-year-old boy whose breath smelled like chocolate milk was my father's absence during my elementary school days. He was locked up most of those years. It was traumatizing for me because even though he was locked up, he was still trying to be a father to me. He wrote me all the time. Whenever I read his letters, it seemed like we were in the same room.

I could hear his voice as if I was in the bunk right above him. He often wrote me about scuffles with other inmates and the subpar prison conditions. Those letters probably had a lot to do with the frequent fights and trouble I got into at school, because I embraced each of my father's encounters as if they were my own.

His prison stories became mine.

My father's experiences in prison were that of a small town. Prison was its own community. Inmates had jobs; inmates went to school. Prison was a business. Some of them used inmates to make furniture; others used inmates to raise chicken and hogs. In my father's run-ins, it was growing fruits and vegetables. It wasn't difficult to guess which crop a prison was growing. My father's prison stints included a surplus of watermelon and way too many sweet potato fries and pies.

The inmates turned fieldworkers who grew these crops were known as the hoe squad. Working in the hoe squad was one of the best jobs in prison because of the hours. They worked for fifty-five minutes a day with a ten-minute break – Monday through Friday – and were off weekends and holidays. And field workers didn't have to go into work on bad weather days.

My father was a fieldworker.

His job, as hinted in the name hoe squad, was to use a hoe to pull up grass to turn the land into dirt. Most times the land my father was working on was so far away from the prison that he couldn't see the building. For the most part, it was all repetitious – groups of inmates slamming their hoes into the ground in unison. But occasionally, a few workers slacked off.

"We're going to stay out here until everybody gets it right," a guard bellowed.

The guard's words were met with grunts and moans of displeasure from the inmates.

"Everybody better make sure they're doing it right," the guard said.

My father was tired. The fifty-five-minute mark was near; everybody was tired.

"Tighten up," my father whispered over to a Mexican guy working next to him.

"Fuck it," the Mexican guy whispered back. "I don't feel like doing no more."

"I'm tired of telling you," my father snapped back. "If I can't get it through your mind, I'mma get it through your body."

My father threw down his hoe, ran up to the Mexican guy and jabbed the Mexican guy in his ear. The Mexican guy fell to the floor, but jumped up quickly with his hoe in his hand.

"Go ahead and take care of it," the guard said to my father and the Mexican guy.

Go ahead and take care of it meant that they could fight, but they couldn't use weapons. The Mexican guy dropped his hoe and he and my father started fighting. After a few minutes of my father standing over the top of the Mexican guy, the guard stopped the fight. When my father wrote me about the fight it sounded petty and pointless. But as his letters continued, I started to get it.

But prison wasn't all guts and glory. For every fight there was friendship. For every heartbreaker there was a broken heart. That friend for my father was Cicero Davis. Cicero was from Port Arthur, Texas. He was in prison for the same reason most black men were – drugs.

Cicero was a basketball player. He played a little college ball, but got caught up in the streets selling drugs. He wasn't a tall guy but had a muscular physique. He had money, too. Cicero kept thousands of dollars on his books but, as part of prison rules, could only use a small amount of that money a month. My father helped him find other things to do with his money.

If girls came to the prison, Cicero made sure my father had one, too. My father talked about Cicero all the time. My father told me about the holiday season that he and Cicero would never forget.

"My mama's coming today," Cicero told my father.

Cicero and my father went back and forth sharing stories about their mothers while Cicero waited to be called to visitation. But Cicero's mother never came.

That night Cicero got word that his mother was killed in a car accident on her way to see him. The news shook everybody. And for a night, prison was a house of mourning. As sad as it was, Cicero's story wasn't the saddest story my father ever told.

Clay Pull's story was the saddest.

Clay was a white guy from a small town right outside of Houston. It was his first prison stint. He was real passive and didn't know the first thing about surviving in prison. My father always taught me that in prison the strong survive and the weak fall to the side. Clay didn't get that memo. He was too friendly. People saw that and took his kindness for weakness.

He wanted to fit in with the white inmates, but was too passive for the skinheads. So he hung out at the domino table with the Black inmates. He didn't know how to play dominoes, but it was sit with the Blacks, be beaten on by the Mexicans or learn how to run with the skinheads.

The Mexicans were always out for Clay. He was a good-looking, clean-skinned white boy and that attracted some of the prison's most ruthless inmates. It started out as favors. Mexican inmates knew Clay was too nice to turn them down so they asked him to buy them things from the commissary. Favors turned into blackmails and threats. The Mexican mafia started pressuring him for money. And when Clay couldn't pay, the imprisoned mafia men found other means of compensation.

"Somebody, call a guard!" Clay yelled as he stumbled out of his cell. He was bleeding and his pants were down.

The Mexicans raped him and beat him.

I wasn't in prison to see it. But my father told the story so well that I thought I was. The stories only got worse, never better. My father had seen so many things that it was hard to imagine how he could continue doing things to land him back in prison. But after a while, it seemed like he was used to prison. Anything outside of prison was foreign. Prison was like a pantry, and my father had spent way too many years on the shelf. All he knew was that pantry.

He found ways to preserve his sanity and make prison feel like home. He put powder on his bed sheets. He saved his best prison uniform for visitation days and church services. He didn't have an iron, but he used to press his clothes with wax that was used to clean floors. He sprayed a little of it on his pants and shirts, dabbed his clothes with water and put them under his mattress until they were dry. The wax and mattress trick made his clothes look dry cleaned. That made him feel normal.

Prison was also the one place he never used drugs.

Towards the end of my fifth grade year, my father was released from prison. Even though I knew it would be tough for my father to recondition himself to the real world, I couldn't help but to hope. In a shoe box, with scraps of paper covered with rap verses were letters full of promises.

From prison, my father went to stay at my grandma's house. For the first month, he kept himself busy with household chores. But he got bored after a while. He couldn't shake the voice in his head. His brain was infected. Addiction was something that no scalpel could take out. He ignored her at first, but as she continued to call, he answered back. I got a call from my grandma about a month and a half into my father's release. She hadn't seen him in a couple of days. I knew then, my father wasn't just an addict; he was a crack head.

I didn't need an eight-year-old boy to tell me that.

TRACK 7

It's been five days. He's never stayed away for more than three days at a time. He hasn't called. Well, he never calls. My grandmother called me earlier in panic, because my father didn't take his high-blood pressure pills with him. Every time I heard my grandmother's voice on the other end, I thought she was going to tell me that my father was found face down in a crack house. It hasn't been more than an hour since she last called.

I didn't know why she was calling again.

"Hello?"

"Hey Nette, what are you doing?"

It was my father. His speech was broken, his words slurred. The foul smell of the streets lingered in his voice. His tone reeked of crack cocaine.

I wasn't prepared for this conversation.

"What do you mean how am I doing? Where have you been? We've been worried sick about you."

"I know. Grandma told me. Man, now I'm here trying to get stuff straight with this parole officer," he nonchalantly said.

"Why, what is he saying?" I sarcastically asked. I knew damn well what his PO was saying.

"He's talking about sending me to another rehab or maybe jail. But I'm not going to jail."

"Why not? You violated parole and you broke the law!"

"Yea, but it's not like I'm out there robbing people."

"Daddy, you might not be out there robbing people, but you robbed me, Boshavar, and Brushaud of a father. You robbed my mama of a husband. I know you don't know this, but a lot of stuff happened to me because you weren't around."

I knew I should've stopped right there. I already said too much. But I was hurt. I skipped past intellect and went straight to my emotions. My voice was in its highest pitch and tears were right around the corner. My father sat on the other end of the line, silent and emotionless.

"Did you know I was molested when I was nine years old?"

"By who?" He demanded to know.

"By Brushaud's friend... the one that just got sentenced to thirty years for molesting his daughter."

"Damn, man," he said, before going completely silent.

"Yea, but I'm okay... I'm good now," I quickly responded. "God brought me through it. I just wanted you to see that the choices you're making affect other people, not just you."

That was partially true. I wanted him to know that his decisions affected all of us. But more than that, I wanted to hurt my father. I wanted to cut him deep. I was always sensitive to my father's feelings. Whenever he and I spoke, we always tip-toed around the truth. We rarely talked about his crack cocaine addiction.

But I was fed up.

Twelve years had passed since I was molested, but I still couldn't help but to wonder if my father's presence could have changed things. He wasn't there to save me when I needed him most. Instead, he was serving a two-year prison sentence for the possession of crack cocaine.

Every time my father got silent, I thought of ways to try to hurt him with my words. I wanted to describe every little detail about the night I was molested. I wanted him to have a vivid picture of what crack cocaine had done to our family, namely me. It was time for him to hear it.

After all, I lived with it every day. It wasn't as gruesome of a story as other stories I'd heard. There was no blood. There were no tears. After the incident, I worked my brain overtime to try to forget that night, so there are still certain things I can't remember. I don't remember the exact date. I always thought it was Christmas Eve or a day very close to it.

But I can't say that with certainty.

I just remember the house being completely silent.

* * *

My mother was sleep in her bedroom, after a long evening of entertaining and cleaning. Brushaud, now a high school sophomore, was dating a girl named Shawnte. She was senior. She was a typical yellow bone

47

– a mixed girl with a bright skin tone and good hair. She and Brushaud were always having problems.

That night was no different.

He fled from our house in the middle of the night, to be with her. From what I could make of the conversation, they were breaking up. Boshavar was sleep on the top bunk bed in the room he and I shared. My younger cousin, Pig, who often spent the night at our house on weekends and any time we were out of school, was asleep in a corner of our room. And I was occupying the bottom bunk bed.

As I did each night, I remember turning on my nightlight. Often times, I had nightmares of Freddy Kruger and other horror films. The nightlight gave me a sense of security. It was late, well after midnight. I should have been sleep, but I was in bed eavesdropping, as I always seemed to do, on Brushaud. He had his own car, so it wasn't uncommon for him to leave at odd hours of the night.

But on this night, he wasn't alone.

Brushaud's good friend, Adrian was spending the night at our house. He was seventeen, just a year older than Brushaud. Adrian and Brushaud had been friends for a long time. He was a friend of the family. Our mothers grew up together and later worked at the same company. I had a crush on a lot of Brushaud's friends. Adrian was one of them. He played basketball, and I liked that.

And he was always nice to me.

Before Brushaud left, he asked Adrian if he wanted to tag along. Adrian declined. A little after Brushaud left, Adrian came into my bedroom. He glanced over at Boshavar and Pig, and then signaled for me to move from the bottom bunk to the floor. I did. He asked if he could turn off my nightlight. With a head nod, I gave him permission to do so.

I won't lie, I was excited.

I was nine.

I couldn't believe an older guy wanted to be in the same room with me instead of hanging out with Brushaud. My brother's friends never gave me that kind of attention. In fact, no man until that night had given me that much attention. For the first time in my life, I felt like I came first.

A man chose me.

As I lay on the floor next to Adrian, he reached over to turn off the nightlight. As the light went out, he kissed me. It wasn't the peck on the lips that I'd once shared with a boy at my elementary school. It was sinful, yet somehow still pleasurable at the same time. I mimicked what his lips did. His hands found a resting spot on the circles on my chest.

My breasts were very small then, but big enough to be noticed. He kissed them and continued down my stomach. Adrian pulled down the little blue shorts I was wearing down, along with my panties. I didn't know what he was doing then, but now I know that his head against my private area was oral sex. There was no climax. I just lay there confused.

And then he stopped.

I thought he was going to leave. But instead, he signaled for me to come near him. He pulled down the

49

white, mesh basketball shorts he was wearing and put my hand on his private area. With my hand in his, he moved my hand up and down. And then he told me to put my mouth on his private area.

As I did, he pushed my head down and his private entered my mouth. I tried several times to pull my head up, but he pushed back down. After about five or ten minutes he let me come up for air. He then kissed me on my lips, pulled up his shorts and left the room. I pulled up my clothes quickly, and hopped back in bed. When I looked over at Pig, I thought I saw his eyes open, but he never said anything.

The little girl in me died that night.

My body and mind had been tampered with, and nothing was ever the same again. I hated myself every day after that night. I just couldn't understand why I didn't scream for help or say anything. As it was happening, I thought about two people – Jesus Christ and my father. But neither one of them came to my rescue that night.

* * *

That's what I wanted to tell him.

But I couldn't tell my father that. I didn't have the heart to hurt him like that. Besides, I blamed myself more than anybody else. I was only a kid, but maybe I acted too grown. I don't know. But that night messed me up. I lost my innocence that night.

I never got it back.

I didn't see Adrian again until I was an adult. When I first saw him, I was confused. A part of me hated him. But there were parts of me that wanted to forgive him.

He was a military soldier by day and a rapper by night. He made music for the ghetto and for the military. I dug that.

His music was selfless, and it made it me feel like that selfish teenager who took advantage of me died and came back a better man. After running into Adrian, he and I talked all the time. He invited me to his shows and he let me in his circle. He asked me to make a song with him. At first, I was hesitant. It seemed awkward and unnatural. But after our first song, it felt right. Those ill thoughts disappeared. I got lost in the music. He did, too. And our love for music produced a friendship.

A few tracks into our friendship, Adrian asked me to be part of his rap dynasty. That day, I saw the sky open up. And so I buried Lady T and morphed into Short Stack. One of Adrian's friends gave me that name Short Stack. It was appropriate. I was short and my body was stacked like a video vixen's.

Adrian and I didn't just make music; we made magic. We spent all of our downtime on stage and in late-night studio sessions. We performed at children's shelters and nightclubs throughout the city. And even though there was always an elephant in the room, I thought the music was big enough to cover it up.

But one night after a studio session, Adrian called me back into his living room just as everyone else was leaving. He asked me for a hug and as we released, he kissed me. I was so caught off guard that I didn't know what to do or how to react. I pulled away as calmly as I knew how and left. As I walked to my car, I replayed the kiss in my head. Was it my fault? Did I ask for that? Adrian and I were so close to going on our first tour. Weeks before that night, Adrian announced that he booked a tour with the military to go to Army bases all around the world. He asked me to go with him. I still wanted to go. But I knew I couldn't. Adrian's kiss had kissed our dreams of ever making it big together goodbye. The next day, Adrian pretended as though the kiss never happened. He asked me to come to his house to finish recording a song. I made up some bogus reason as to why I couldn't. My mind was already made up. I loved music and I loved our potential, but I refused to be humiliated and sexually assaulted all over again. I never saw Adrian again. Days after the kiss, he sent me a series of confessional text messages. He admitted that he not only remembered that night twelve years before, but that he wanted to relive it. He gloated at the memories. He said it wasn't molestation, because it was mutual. Age didn't matter. I kept his messages in my phone for weeks. I wanted to go to the cops. I wanted to tell my family.

But I was too embarrassed.

I knew what people would say about me. I chose to make to music with the same person who molested me. It didn't make sense. So I didn't do anything. When my family asked me why I stopped recording music with Adrian, I lied to them. I told them he was in trouble with the military and that I didn't want any part of it. That was true. He was in trouble with the military, but that's not why we parted ways.

After that, I never talked about Adrian. I swore

I never would. But today, it seemed necessary. I wanted to give my father a wake-up call. I wanted to say something that would trigger a little emotion, a little uneasiness and a lot of discomfort. I thought a discussion, like the one we were having, would be more than enough to make him stop using drugs.

"Nette, you've said a lot. I think I'm going to go," he said.

"Okay Dad," I said. "I guess I'll just talk to you later."

"Yea, okay."

And just like that, he hung up.

My father never called back that day like he said he would. I didn't expect him to. But I at least hoped that he heard the hurt and pain in my voice. Maybe it would be enough. About a week later, I called my grandmother. She talked me up about the weather and things she'd seen on the news.

"Is my daddy there?" I interrupted.

"He's gone baby. He was supposed meet with his parole officer yesterday. He said he was catching the bus and he never came back."

There wasn't much conversation after she said that. We hurried off the phone, ending with words of encouragement and 'I love you.' I kept my composure while she was on the phone. My grandmother was a worrier. I didn't want to add to that. But when we hung up, I went to my bedroom and cried like a baby.

And as always, I wrote.

TRACK 8

"Y'all niggas know that little check y'all getting ain't gone be enough to pay for no school clothes," Ernest said, as he offered a seat to four teenage boys. "Y'all niggas need to flip that money."

That summer of 1975, Ernest introduced my father to weed as if she was a virgin longing to have her cherry popped. Ernest was the project's weed man. But looking at him, you'd never know it. He was a college kid, on a football scholarship. Selling weed was his side hustle.

Ernest knew everything there was to know about the drug game.

"Make that shit look pretty for the customers," Ernest yelled.

My father was a rookie. He was young and still wet behind the ears. The closest he'd been to weed was a peek he got at his older brother Bernard sneaking to smoke a joint behind his mama's house in the projects. He was working a summer gig with a local youth program, making two hundred dollars every two weeks.

But he was intrigued by Ernest's hustle and he clung to it.

It didn't take my father long to score his first pound of weed. A pound sold for $125. Pounds were manicured and broken down into joints and four-finger-lid bags. No one in the projects owned a scale to weigh the weed, so they used a four-finger-lid method to make bags. My father stuffed weed into a small plastic bag until it was the length and width of four of his fingers.

The bags sold for ten dollars each, and joints went for fifty cents. My father spent an hour or two a day rolling one hundred joints.

Getting rid of the work was easy.

Ernest had built up enough street cred for the both of them to make money. They only sold to people in the projects, so the chances of selling to a snitch or a cop were close to none. That summer, my father transitioned from junior high to high school, and from just selling weed to smoking it. He started sampling his product. And sampling progressed into weekend-long binges.

At first my father was selling weed to make a little extra summer cash. But he continued smoking and selling weed well into his freshman year. Everybody smoked weed in the 1970s. At his high school, there were two kinds of kids – project kids and house kids.

The project kids had first dibs on weed because every project had a weed man. Most of the house kids didn't have a regular weed man in their neighborhood. So my father sold to the house kids. Joints were easier to hide, quicker to sale, and the consequences for getting caught were lower. He had only one rule: Never sell a bag of weed at school.

The longer he sold, the craftier he got, and the more risks he took.

* * *

"Hide that shit. Coach is coming," another student yelled back to my father as he tried to pass him a joint.

"You know I saw that right, Bruce?"

"I'll throw it out, Coach. Can you just let it slide this one time?"

"I should call your mama, but I don't want you to get in trouble. So, let's make a deal. You come out for the track team and I won't tell your mama."

"Okay, Coach. You got it."

* * *

My father was a standout athlete. He was coming off an incredible eighth-grade year in just about every sport. At the end of his eighth-grade year he was awarded "Best Athlete." But winning a race, catching a football, or dunking a basketball never held my father's interest.

He outgrew that world. High school sports didn't mix well with his new lifestyle – sex, smoking weed, and drinking cheap liquor. Two weeks later, my father quit the track team.

"Call my mama. Tell her. I don't care."

"Well alright, I'm gonna call her."

And as promised, the track coach called his mother. The consequences didn't matter.

My father had been tightrope walking between sin and purity since he was thirteen. The summer following his thirteenth birthday was the same summer my father's little league team won the city championship.

After the game, the team went to the icehouse that used to sit where the McDonald's now sits on the corner of Walters Street.

"Y'all can get whatever y'all want," the coach said, as he reached for an eight-ounce can of Schlitz malt liquor.

The coach went around in a circle, asking each kid what they wanted. My father, who was peeking over the heads of two of his teammates, couldn't take his eyes off the beer can. He was mesmerized by the water trickling down the sides of the can.

"Grape soda," one kid yelled.

"Orange soda," said another kid.

"Whatchu you want, Bruce?"

"I want what you got," my father answered.

"If you turn it up, you better kill it," the coach told my father as he tossed him the eight-ounce can of beer.

Everyone at the icehouse stared at my father. He gave a quick, nervous smile, pulled the cap back, pressed the can against his lips, and gutted the beer as if he'd been drinking all his life. Word got back to his mother then too, but my father feared few things and even fewer people.

* * *

By the time the track coach called his mother, it was too late. He was hooked on getting high. But back then, he was still in control. He continued going to school. He never played sports again. But he took up singing and even entered a few high school talent shows.

He was a poor man's Lionel Richie.

He sung his way onto high school and nightclub

stages as the lead singer with The Futuristics, a local teenaged funk and soul band. My father made twenty-five dollars a show to perform funk and soul classics in raunchy old night clubs. And after every show, the group smoked a joint. Most of the members went home after a joint or two. But after each high, my father yearned for the next one.

Weed wasn't enough.

One night after a show, one of the other group members pulled out a little square sheet. The square sheet was a little thicker than notebook paper. He put the small square in his mouth, and pulled another one out of his pocket. He offered it to my father.

That night, my father put a drug other than weed into his body for the first time. That little square was LSD, a potent hallucinogenic drug. The drug came as a square sheet and in the pill form. The pill was orange and nicknamed "Orange Sunshine." It was about the size of a baby aspirin. If he was getting high with at least three other people, they took four-way hits.

A four-way hit was a larger sheet with enough LSD to get four people high. LSD kept him amped up for eight to ten hours at a time. He was cockier when he was under the influence of LSD. And if he got drunk off liquor or high off weed, LSD sustained his buzz. He was altering between a drug-infused singer, a high school student, and a father-to-be.

Somewhere in between getting high and serenading women twice his age, my father was dating my mother. My mother was a house kid. She was one of six girls. Her father was a preacher and her mother played the piano at a local Baptist church. They lived on Blaine Street, which was no more than a five-or-ten-minute drive from the projects my father lived in. My mother was a year older than my father.

On most days after school, they went to my father's house in the projects. It was a three-bedroom apartment. My dad shared a room with his older brothers, Boyd and Bernard. My dad had been having sex since he was thirteen years old, so my mother knew what came with hanging out at his house.

My parents didn't practice safe sex.

During my father's junior year of high school and my mother's senior year, my mother found out she was pregnant. The news meant nothing to my father. And my mother was young. She wasn't ready to be a mother.

She had an abortion.

My father never talked about the abortion. He continued doing what he was doing. After about three years with The Futuristics, my father left the group. He was almost a man now; nearly eighteen years old. He was tired of making twenty-five dollars a show. Selling ten-dollar-weed bags and fifty-cent joints wasn't cutting it either.

TRACK 9

"Is anybody sitting here?" I asked as I pointed to a seat just beside an old Mexican lady.

She shook her head no.

I could tell she didn't speak much English and I was glad. I hated bus stations. Even more so, I hated conversing with people at bus stations. Whenever I did, I felt like I was sitting on a toilet in a public restroom talking to the person in the stall next to me.

Bus stations were disgusting. The one in downtown smelled of must and pierced ears. Before I moved to Omaha, I worked in downtown San Antonio for more than four years, but that didn't change how I felt about the area.

It felt unsafe.

* * *

My boss, Jamie, was very understanding. In this case, I needed her to be. If she had said no, I would've left anyway. I loved my job, but my father came first. Besides, my father was the only reason I got that job. Before serving time at state prisons, my father spent days, weeks, and sometimes months at the county jail.

There were few things to like about the county jail; one of them was being able to read the local newspaper.

He read it as often as he could.

My father talked about journalism and the power of writing in just about every letter he wrote to me. I grew to appreciate the art at a young age, and by age fourteen I was sure I wanted to be a writer. I wrote music, poetry and stories that made people laugh, smile and sometimes cry.

I never told my father about my love for music. Music was always a little forbidden to me. Growing up I always heard people say that music was at the root of my father's addiction. My mother said my father sang at nightclubs that were much too vulgar for a teenaged boy. My mother always thought he was exposed to too much in those clubs. So when I wrote my father, I only talked about the poetry and short-story-writing side.

As I got older and was into my first year at college, my father suggested I write to my local newspaper. His favorite writer was Cary Clack, a columnist who was a modern day Martin Luther King Jr. with a pen. He reported the positive Black stories; the ones that would otherwise fall into a recycling bin.

During the second semester of my freshman year, I took my father's advice. I sent Cary an email. Through a series of back and forth emails with Cary and his boss, I was offered a ten-dollar-an-hour summer internship as an editorial assistant. That same month, my father was arrested for possession of crack cocaine. He read about the good news in a letter. By then, I should've been used to it being that way but I wasn't.

Even in my father's absences, I felt like I was doing everything for him. In my younger days when I was playing basketball, I wrote his name on my headbands. When I graduated from high school, I pretended he was there. And this time, I vowed to write as though he was reading.

I was an editorial assistant, not a reporter. My job was a clerical one. It consisted of answering phones, writing news briefs and occasionally, going to get food for the editors. But that wasn't enough for me. Sure, I was a nobody; a nineteen-year-old freshman who wasn't even crafty enough to write a resume. But I needed clips. I wanted to send my father a news article with my byline.

Within a month on the job, I got my first byline. I wrote about a local church that held services in sign language for the deaf. I never told my father this, but I was so scared that I asked my mother to attend the service with me.

After my first byline, I was a regular in the metro section. The summer internship turned into a full-time position. I wrote about everything from a homeless community's fight to save their makeshift homes, to an aspiring rapper in San Antonio. No matter what I wrote about it, I always tried to make it lyrical. When I read my stories out loud, I wanted it to sound like music.

Each time my byline appeared in the paper, it felt like performance. My stories became songs. And I got lost in them. I loved it. I loved my bosses and co-workers. They even supported my rap career. Two of my editors called me by my rap name, Short Stack.

One year at the paper, I wrote a rap about working in the newsroom. It was called "More News". I performed it at a work talent show and won third place. The judges, with the exception of one, didn't know the first thing about entertainment. A comedian who wasn't funny won first place. And my editor Nora beat me out with her Lady Gaga impression. But after the talent show, she gave me her second place prize and she took my third place one. The next day, the lyrics to my song were posted on an internal website so everyone who worked at the newspaper could have a copy.

That was my rock star moment.

We were family. That's not to say that everybody was cool. Just like with family, some people were messy and others just got on my nerves. But there were three people I trusted just as much as I did my real family.

Regina, who was my first supervisor, was the sister I never had. She was hilarious with a touch of crazy, but she taught me everything there was to know about the job. She had the scoop on everything – who was getting fired and who was sleeping with whom.

Vince was the only Black reporter in the metro section. He had a knack for writing feature stories. He was like a father to me. He was a little older than my parents and was in the latter years of working after having served more than twenty years in the Air Force. He and I ate lunch together at least two or three times a week. And he never hit on me, not once.

Michelle was different. We were like hands to a body. I was the left, and she was the right. She covered crime. I was her ear to the streets. But she never took advantage of me. If I ever helped with a story, she always gave me a contributing line. She wasn't out to be the best the writer. She just wanted the newspaper to have the best reporting.

Because she covered crime, I was able to help her. Most people call it media bias or stereotyping, but believe it or not a lot of Black people kill Black people.

Sadly, I knew most of those Black people.

Michelle and I talked about a lot of different things concerning the Black community – religion, sports, family, violence and education. She wanted to understand the struggle just as much as I did.

Somehow, all those conversations lead to one about my father. Everyone I worked with knew about my father. Maybe I should have been, but I wasn't ashamed of him. I wasn't embarrassed by his addiction; I was hurt by it.

Michelle was a good listener and offered good advice. As a way of thanking me for passing on street knowledge, Michelle offered me something else. As a cop reporter, Michelle had access to a criminal records database. Using a first and last name and a date of birth, she could retrieve someone's criminal history.

I shouldn't have flirted with the idea. I should've dismissed it. But I needed to know if my father's criminal history was stored in that database. I had no reason to pry. My father wasn't one to hold his tongue.

He always gave it to me raw and uncut, whether it was the truth about crack quarrels with other addicts or sleeping with other women while he was married to my mother. And even though I knew some things about my father, there were other things I was curious about but didn't want to know. Curiosity kills a cat.

I asked Michelle to look it up.

His rap sheet was pages and pages long. There were drug charges after drug charges. But at the top of his record were burglary and purse snatching charges.

He never mentioned those.

* * *

The bus station was only a few blocks from the newspaper, so I left work fifteen minutes before my father's bus was to arrive. I was into my second year as a full-time editorial assistant at the paper, so I figured it had been close to three years since I last saw my father as a free man. He was forty-eight-years-old, now. I kept telling myself that somewhere in between forty-five and forty-eight years old my father had to have changed.

"Excuse me, what time is the bus from Huntsville scheduled to arrive?" I asked a lady standing behind a counter in front of the bus station.

"That should be the next bus."

His bus was scheduled to arrive at seven thirty.

It was eight o'clock.

We were on a strict schedule. From San Antonio, Brushaud and I had to drive him to a halfway house in Austin. Austin was only an hour away, but my father had to be at the halfway house by ten o'clock.

I was tired of sitting down, so I went outside and stood not too far from where the buses pulled up and off from.

"How long have you been waiting?" a lady asked me

as I stood against the window of the station.

"For an hour," I said as I pressed my wallet against my chest.

It was dark outside, and women were just as much cons as men were.

"I've been here for two hours," the lady said. "I'm waiting on my son's bus from Huntsville."

"I'm waiting on that bus, too... for my dad."

This lady seemed nice. She was Mexican and probably in her late fifties. She didn't say much else about her son; only that she was glad he was coming home.

I didn't ask her any questions, either.

"Here comes the bus," she said.

The bus pulled up a little after eight thirty.

One after another, Mexican men covered in tattoos stepped off the bus. After fifteen or so heads, my father stepped off the bus.

"Daddy," I called over to my father as he stepped down.

There he was in the flesh, bald headed and at least fifty pounds heavier than I last saw him. He was wearing a red collar shirt and a pair of blue jeans that were at least two sizes too big.

"Nette!"

My father hugged and kissed me on the forehead as we walked to the car.

We went to my grandma's house first. Brushaud was supposed to meet us there. My father wanted to see my grandma, too, and to gather up some of his old clothes. But my father couldn't fit into any of his old clothes. Brushaud offered to take him to Wal-Mart on the way to Austin. My father said his goodbyes to my grandma and we left. The ride to Austin was cool. My father humored us with prison stories. He was a good storyteller.

We all were.

We stopped at a Wal-Mart right outside of Austin. My father didn't know what size pants he wore, but we knew it was in the forties. He got a pack of T-shirts, jogging pants, two pair of jeans and some basketball shorts.

"You know what I need," my father told Brushaud. "I need some razors."

My father was such a kid when it came to shopping. He wanted everything he saw and everything he could think of. Brushaud went to get the razors while I helped my father pick out a belt.

"I ought to just put this belt on," my father said.

"Daddy," I quickly responded. "You bet not steal that belt."

"Man, I'm not finsta pay for this belt. I could just put it over these pants I got."

He put the belt around his waist and walked to the front of the store. I didn't know what to say. He was my father, not my child. He was an adult. I knew he was wrong, but it wasn't my place.

"Daddy, what about...," I said as we stood in the checkout line. Before I could finish my sentence, he cut me off with a hand gesture that signaled for me to shut up.

As we checked out and walked to the car, my father

lagged behind.

"Daddy stole that belt he got on," I whispered to Brushaud, low enough so that my father couldn't hear me.

"You lying!" Brushaud said.

That's was an expression of speech. He knew I wasn't lying. I didn't want to be known as a snitch, but I couldn't believe my father stole a ten-dollar belt from Wal-Mart on the same day he was released from prison.

As soon as my father made it to the car, Brushaud sent him back into Wal-Mart to pay for the belt.

"Just tell them you forgot to pay for it," Brushaud told him.

My father looked at me and then at Brushaud.

"Daddy, you gotta do this," Brushaud pleaded. "This will make you a better person."

When my father got back to the car I couldn't even look his way. He knew I was the rat.

"You did the right thing, Nette," my father turned and told me.

But that was just it – I struggled with right and wrong when it came to my father. Right would have been to stop him before he ever walked out the store with the belt. But right would have also been to have kept my mouth shut.

Integrity was right.

Loyalty was right, too.

On the short ride from Wal-Mart to the halfway house, Brushaud used every movie line and inspirational quote he could think of to motivate my father.

"What we do in life echoes in eternity," Brushaud

said as he looked over at my father. "I got that from my favorite movie, Gladiator."

My father just sat in the passenger's seat, listening and nodding. I felt bad for him. Physically, he was strong, but mentally, he couldn't lift a feather. He spent his prison time pumping weights and doing pushups and sit-ups to get big. But prison didn't offer anything for his mind. It hurt to know that about him, but it was true.

We got to the halfway house close to midnight. The security guards at the house were upset, but they still let my father check in. They told us we were welcome to visit him on weekends and ushered us out the door. I looked back at my father and waved goodbye. He promised to call as soon as he could.

His calls were sporadic, so I missed a lot of them. He left me the most depressing voicemail messages, saying things like he was sorry to bother me. It was hard to listen to them, because I always felt that he called me when he was at his weakest. It's as if he sought me for strength.

"Hey Nette, it's me," my father said to my voicemail. "I'm out for a doctor's appointment so I just called to see what you were doing. But you didn't answer your phone. I guess I'll try to call you back. Bye."

That was the last voicemail I got from him before receiving a call from Brushaud. My father's parole officer told Brushaud that my father failed to return to the halfway house and that a warrant for his arrest had been issued.

We waited by our phones to hear from my father.

Days passed.

A week later, my father called Brushaud from a pay phone near a bus station in Austin. Brushaud could barely understand my father as he mumbled through sentences, but Brushaud gathered enough information to locate the bus station.

Brushaud wanted to be sure my father was there so he called a friend who lived in Austin to drive by the bus station.

"Are you Bruce?" my brother's friend asked a man as she tapped his shoulder.

"Yes," my father responded in a low tone.

"Brushaud sent me."

My father was slumped over at the bus station, covered in mud. His shoes were torn at the seams and his feet were swollen and bulging out from the soles of the shoes.

Brushaud's friend waited at the station with my father until Brushaud got there. My father slept on the car ride back to San Antonio. When they arrived, we didn't know what to do. We didn't want to see him go back to jail.

So this time, we chose loyalty.

He spent the night at Brushaud's apartment.

TRACK 10

"Drop me off right up there where that man is standing and circle around the block," my father instructed. "By the time you come back, I'll be ready."

"Time flies when you're having fun."

It's funny how that old cliché always proves true. What's even funnier is how time sits still when you're not. I didn't want to do it. I knew it was wrong. But if I didn't supply it, someone else would.

So I dropped him off at a one-story house, not too far from the Wheatley Courts – an Eastside housing project. There was a short, round-bodied Mexican man standing near the front door. My father trotted through the front yard and onto the porch. He looked back toward the car, gave me a head nod, and disappeared into the house.

I drove slowly.

Scattered shades of blue and red police sirens were in my rearview mirror. Two cop cars were parked side-by-side in an abandoned lot at the end of the street. I sat up straight, lowered my music, and glanced at the speedometer of my Saturn to make sure I was driving no faster than twenty miles per hour.

My run-ins with the cops were minimal to none, but I still didn't trust them. San Antonio housed too many crooked cops. You could get caught with a little weed, but later be charged with a dope case. And sometimes, if you had a little weed you could be released.

I looked down at my wedding band and then at my son's empty car seat. It was well-passed 6 p.m. I normally picked Jason Jr. up by 5:30 p.m. every weekday. But today when I pulled up at my grandma's house, my father ran out to the car.

"Nette, I need a favor," he started out. "I need you to run me somewhere real quick."

"Okay."

My father ran back into the house to tell my grandma that I was giving him a ride to the store. She insisted I leave Jason Jr. with her until we got back.

"Do you want to go to H-E-B?" I asked as soon as my father got into the car.

H-E-B was the closest grocery store to my grandma's house. My father enjoyed walking around grocery stores, starting conversations with random women. He always flirted with the most unattractive women. And when I asked him about it, he said everybody needed love.

"Man, Nette, I really don't need to go to the store," my father said. "I need you to take me to get some weed."

My brain immediately said no. I couldn't believe he asked me to take him to buy weed. I was a Christian, a wife, and a mother. I was a Sunday regular at church.

My family and friends dubbed me mother and wife of the year. I wore those crowns humbly. His request went against everything I stood for.

And even so, my heart said yes.

More weed meant less crack. I knew that rationale wouldn't fair over with my husband or my mother. But part of understanding my father and what motivated him to do the things he did lied in situations like these. That day, I felt like he was on the verge of slipping out of my grandma's back door and back onto the streets to use crack cocaine. And I felt like he was begging me to catch him before he slipped.

"Okay," I agreed.

"I know what you're thinking, Nette."

My father could hear the shame and fear in my voice. I smiled to lighten the situation. I felt so uncomfortable, but I knew I had to do this. As we drove down my grandma's street, I searched for anything to take me away. I cranked up the volume of my car radio and started rapping along with rap songs to drown out my thoughts.

* * *

I went to a college in Missouri for two years. My second year there, I got involved with a guy from Kansas City. Langston was the greatest mistake of my life. The warning signs and red lights were there. But I ignored them.

He was a handsome guy, but he was covered in pain. His mother died when he was eleven years old. After her passing, he started smoking wet – weed dipped in embalming fluid. He was a year younger than me, and had recently been released from a youth detention center. He wasn't in school and was days removed from being fired from a fast food eatery. He didn't smoke wet anymore, but he was a weed head and a bit of a drinker.

Still, somewhere behind his discolored lips, big afro, and his potty mouth was a person who needed help. I wanted to be that person. But I was just as broken as he was, and the blind can't lead the blind.

It bothered me that he smoked, but I tolerated it. He knew my father's story, so he never offered me a hit. Some nights, I flirted with the idea of smoking. But I was too scared of becoming my father.

"You're a lame," Langston and his friends used to joke.

Langston said I was the only young person he knew who didn't smoke weed. I was proud of that. He and his friends smoked weed every night. I always sat curled up on Langston's couch, staring at Scarface posters trying to pretend the smoke didn't bother me. And most nights went like that. But one night, while at Langston's apartment, my grandma called.

"Yo' daddy is about to run my blood pressure up," she said.

"What happened?" I asked.

"He done went there and got arrested. He's in jail baby."

"Do you know what he got arrested for?"

"Drugs."

After I got off the phone with my grandma, I ran outside and started punching the brick walls outside of Langston's apartment.

"I hate my life," I screamed at the top of my lungs. "I hate my father."

Langston walked up to me, hugged me and guided me to the parking lot. His best friend, a lesbian girl who played basketball at the college I went to, was parked near the front of the parking lot. Langston got into the passenger's seat of her old, white Durango and I got in the back seat.

The lesbian girl lit a blunt and passed it to Langston.

"Let me hit it," I said.

He laughed and passed it back to her.

"Let me hit it!"

"She's wolfing," Langston said as the lesbian girl reached back to give me the blunt. "She know she ain't bout to smoke."

I grabbed the blunt and put it to my mouth. I had seen Langston do it a million times, but I still didn't know how to smoke weed.

"Just inhale and exhale," he told me.

And so I did.

My throat burned a little bit, and then came a cough. Langston and his friend laughed at me. But I tried again. I pressed the blunt to my lips, inhaled and exhaled. We passed it back and forth until it was merely ashes. On our walk back to Langston's apartment, I pretended to be high. I laughed loudly and talked even louder.

But weed didn't have that effect on me. The situation made me feel stupid. I was still mad at my father, and even more upset with myself. On my way home from Langston's apartment, I thanked God for sparing me. And because he did, I vowed to never have anything to do with weed again. But I was willing to break that promise for my father. I figured that if God truly knew my heart, he would understand.

* * *

As I circled around the block waiting for my father's head to peek out of the house, something felt wrong. I saw police officers glaring at me from the seats of their police cars. It never occurred to me that repeatedly circling a block was suspicious. As I got closer to the house, I saw my father shake the Mexican's man hand and walk my way. I sank into the driver's seat of my Saturn just as I had three years ago.

As I waited for my father to walk to the car, I started rapping the same lyrics I wrote three years ago, "When the one man that she loves has done her wrong, Promising to stop and be a better father, Yet tip-toeing out to pawn the VCR, Out three days, that's 72 hours, Crazy to see how much food he devours, Gulping down vinegar to clean out his system, She runs to the door, I guess she missed him..."

With a police siren roaring behind us, I hurried my father to get into the car and I blacked out.

TRACK 11

I shouldn't have been surprised when I saw my father sitting at my grandma's kitchen table drinking a glass of vinegar.

He wasn't afraid to try new things.

He used to tell my grandma to rub WD-40 on her aching knees. And if that wasn't enough, he thought bathing in Clorox was the ultimate cleanser.

* * *

The moments are few, but there was a time when my father worked. In 1983, he worked as a houseman at a hotel off N. E. Loop 410 – a highway not too far from the San Antonio International Airport. My father was lucky to get the job. He had been recently released from jail on bond and was awaiting trial on burglary charges.

My father worked nights – eight hours shifts with a one-hour lunch break. He brought his lunch most of the time. On nights that he didn't, he went to lunch with his co-worker, Daryl. Daryl was middle-aged white guy. He had blonde, hippy-like hair and wore a dirty mustache. He smoked way too many Marble cigarettes.

He and my father seemed like an unlikely pair, but they shared one common interest – drugs. My father mostly popped pills and smoked weed. Daryl used crystal meth. Not many black people used crystal meth. It was primarily known as a white person's drug because no one sold crystal meth in projects.

That didn't stop my father from trying it.

"Wanna go to my house for lunch?" Daryl asked my father.

Daryl didn't live too far from the hotel. He was married and didn't have any children. Both he and his wife used crystal meth. When they walked into the house, Daryl pulled out a little white package. He snorted a line and then gave my father a line. My father snorted it. It burned bad. He had a medicinal taste in his throat. Within thirty seconds all five of my father's senses intensified.

When my father returned to work, he was high. It was a different high than he'd ever experienced. This high made him work harder. He swept every leaf off the hotel's parking lot. He cleaned so much that he was sweating. My father's co-workers had to make him to stop sweeping.

My father liked that feeling.

He started going to Daryl's house regularly. My father snorted a line or two every time he went to his house. But after a while, my father wanted more than a line or two. Once when my father was at Daryl's house, he saw Daryl and his wife shooting up crystal meth. My father saw the look on Daryl's wife's face and knew he had to try it.

"Let me get it like that," my father told Daryl.

My father shot up for the first time.

His throat was hot. The hair on his head was sticking up. My father loved it. If crystal meth had been sold in black areas, it probably would have hit worse than crack did. My father said crystal meth made him feel the best. Crack was like Nas; he was a good rapper who could make you bob your head.

But meth was like Waka Flocka; he got you out of your seat.

But after my father quit working at the hotel, he lost contact with Daryl. By then, my father was looking for a fix. He needed something to replace what crystal meth had been to him. He went back to his old stomping grounds and crystal meth wasn't there.

Crack cocaine was.

* * *

My father straggled into my grandma's house covered in dirt and must. As usual, he took a long bath, shaved and brushed his teeth. He slept that night as though he was haunted by the things he'd done before he laid down.

But none of us dare say a word.

The next morning when I saw him drinking that glass of vinegar I didn't know what he was doing.

"What are you drinking, Daddy?" I asked.

"Vinegar."

"Why?"

"I gotta meet with my parole officer tomorrow," my father began. "Nothing cleans out your system like vinegar."

I didn't know how he knew that. More so, I didn't know how my father convinced himself to drink a glass of vinegar. My grandma never said anything. Neither did I.

I just grabbed a pen, some paper and nine dominoes.

"Are we playing ten to get in?" I asked.

"Nope," my father replied. "All money is good money."

* * *

A few years later, I Googled the words "uses for vinegar" and more than 131 uses for vinegar came back. Believe it or not, but vinegar was indeed a cleanser. Almost all of the uses for vinegar were for cleaning purposes.

But my father had put so much filth into his body – beer, weed, pills, LSD, crystal meth, heroin and crack cocaine. Not even vinegar, with all its cleansing power, could cleanse his system.

That urine test he took for his parole officer came back dirty.

TRACK 12

"That's it!" my mother cried out to an empty room. She called into work sick that day.

My mother spent the day crying and reliving the shattered memories that led up to this day. It was over.

She knew it.

* * *

"Where did Bruce go?" my Aunt Tandy asked my mother.

"He went to the car to go smoke," my mother replied.

"You know," my Aunt Tandy started out. "That's not a good start to a marriage."

While my father was in the car smoking weed with his long-time friends Billy and Lil' Brother, my mother was entertaining guests at their wedding reception.

My parents got married eight months after Brushaud was born. They thought it was the right thing to do. My mother was raised in the church, and my father wanted to make her an honest woman, or so he said.

They got married in the pastor's study at Mount

Sinai Baptist Church. It wasn't too far from the neighborhood my mother grew up. My mother was only twenty. My father was nineteen. Since they didn't have a traditional wedding ceremony, my father's mother threw them a reception in the Sutton Homes. Everyone was there; my mother's and my father's families, their friends and the project-housing residents.

My father was high the whole time.

Maybe that should have been a sign, but my mother was so devoted to my father that she ran past it. Lopsided-devotion was the story of their marriage. No matter what my father did, my mother forgave and forgot. Nine years into their marriage, right after Boshavar was born, everything went downhill. My father had been using drugs for five years, but he'd reached his lowest. Prison and rehab was more of a home to my father than our house ever was.

It was the same ole' routine – my mother would bail my father out of jail if she could or keep money on his books if she couldn't.

We were barely making it.

My mother's paychecks were dwindling faster than my father's physique after a three-day high. It was easier to see him behind bars or stuck between walls that weren't ours. At least like that, he couldn't pawn our stuff.

My father pawned and sold everything – our TV, vacuum cleaner, radios, and even pictures on the wall. He pawned our TV so many times that my mother wrote "Do Not Pawn" on the side of the TV. He even sold the food out of our refrigerator and the clothes out of our closets. If my mother bought us new clothes, she had to take the price tags off right away, fold them and stuff them in dresser drawers.

He took anything that looked new.

Boshavar and I were too young to understand the effects. We didn't notice the missing clothes and appliances. All we remembered were the horsey rides on my father's legs. At that age – three and six – kids are selfish and self-absorbed.

But Brushaud wasn't.

He was only getting older and less tolerant.

The same year Brushaud entered junior high, my father headed off to a prison in Kyle, Texas to serve a three-year sentence. He caught another drug case.

We were all sad to see him go, and we still felt relief.

It took us an hour to drive to Kyle, but my mother made that drive every weekend.

Most of the visits were awkward. My father seemed disinterested and unconcerned with anything going on outside of prison. He only wanted to talk about money on his books and the poor prison conditions.

But my mother kept on visiting him. She believed that in time my father would get better. She was the only one who believed that.

While my father was away in Kyle, my mother was back home trying to get her credit straight. She was making more money now – $45,000 a year. And she promised Brushaud that by the time he entered high school, she would move us out of the Rivera Apartments and into a house.

Brushaud's three years of junior high school flew

by quick. And as promised, the end of my brother's eighth grade year rolled around and my mother started looking for houses. The summer following Brushaud's eighth grade year, we moved into a one-story house on the Northeast side.

For Brushaud, it was a new start. For me and Boshavar, it was what we saw on the movies. For my mother, it was empty without my father. Even though she found the house without him, she was hoping a new house and a new area would make things better.

My father made parole days after my mother closed on the house. As part of his parole, my father was assigned to a halfway house for sixty days. After that, he could come home.

"You want to go see the house?" my mother eagerly asked.

My father could come and go from the halfway house as he pleased as long as he made curfew.

My father nodded.

My mother was so excited and proud of the house she chose.

"I saw it," my father said as my mother pulled into the driveway. "Let's go to the Flea Market."

"Don't you want to see the inside?" she asked.

"No, I trust you."

My mother pulled out of the driveway and headed toward the Flea Market. She didn't say too much after that.

"Oh yeah," my father said sarcastically. "You did real good."

My mother never asked my father why he didn't

want to see the house. A few days later, it was like that incident never happened.

The halfway house staff gave my father permission to drive a car to go look for a job.

We finally had a reliable car. It wasn't fancy, but that two-door Cavalier was better than our last car. Our last car smoked so much that when my mother drove the car, it looked like gray clouds had fallen out of the sky.

My mother told my father that after she dropped us off at school, he could use her car to look for a job. He was scheduled to check in at the halfway house after a few hours of job searching. After that, he had permission to pick my mother up from work and have her drop him back off at the halfway house.

My father never checked in at the halfway house.

A staff at the house called my mom to let her know he never came back. My mother thought he lost track of time, but was sure he would be there to pick her up from work.

He never came.

My father's friend Billy – the same Billy my father used to smoke with – worked at the beverage company with my mother. He didn't smoke anymore. He volunteered to go look for my father. Another co-worker gave my mother, my brothers, and me a ride home. When we walked into the house, the VCR was gone.

"If you allow him to come to this house, then I'm moving in with Grandma," Brushaud said angrily.

"There's no way…" my mother said before tears cut

her off.

My mother was so hurt. On one hand, she loved my father and didn't want to give up on him. On the other hand, there was no way my mother would allow any of us to move out. If she hadn't had us, she would've stuck it out with my father. The one thing she always said was that she would never let my father's addiction ruin our family.

It already had.

I think she was just waiting on one of us to say something.

After we were all in bed, my mother sat in the living room staring at the empty space where the VCR once was. She felt as empty as that space. My mother had suffered more than all of us. But that night it wasn't about her. It was about her choice. She knew she had to choose – us or him.

It broke her heart to leave my father, but she chose us.

TRACK 13

My father was unresponsive, except for occasional outburst about how sorry he was and how that halfway house was no good for him.

Brushaud ignored most of it.

Of the three of us – Boshavar, Brushaud, and me – Brushaud got the worse end of the deal. He was the oldest. My father used to leave Brushaud at parks and movie theaters and everywhere else if he got a craving for crack. One time, my father left him at a park on the south end of New Braunfels Street.

"I'll be right back," he told Brushaud.

Brushaud shook his head and continued playing. My father never came back.

Brushaud walked to the first house he saw. A Mexican woman answered the door and let Brushaud use her phone. The only number he knew was my Aunt Tandy's.

He was just six-years-old.

But Brushaud was a man now. I'm sure the past still hurt, but we were all my father had. Brushaud knew that. He refused to send my father to jail on an infected left foot and an unreliable right one. My father's feet were swollen and covered in blisters. The bottom of his feet burned as he hobbled from the car to Brushaud's apartment.

His thighs were irritated and bruised by once-wet blue jeans rubbing against his legs as he ran through alleys to get away from Austin policemen. He walked in once-wet shoes and clothes for nearly two days.

He wasn't fit for jail. Jail healthcare was horrible. At the jails and prisons my father was housed at, staph infections spread more commonly than the common cold. Jail wasn't safe, either. If something popped off, my father wouldn't have been able to defend himself if he couldn't even stand up straight.

On the way to Brushaud's house, Brushaud picked up some Mexican food. My father scarfed down enchilada after enchilada. Then he showered and went to sleep. He slept nearly two days straight – only waking up to use the bathroom and occasionally eat.

Over those two days, Brushaud decided that his house was the best place for my father. My father had been in prison for four years, so he didn't know where Brushaud lived. The area looked foreign to my father, but Alamo Heights was just a hop, skip and a jump from downtown.

But my father didn't know that.

And even if he figured it out, it wouldn't have mattered. My father was in no condition to run the streets. Besides, there was a warrant for his arrest.

Brushaud's house was the safest place. Brushaud was in regular contact with my father's parole officer. He pretended as though he was just as concerned about my father's whereabouts as his PO was.

My father's PO trusted Brushaud.

* * *

I've always heard people say that all Black people play sports. I grew up believing all Black people played dominoes.

"Quarter in that order," my father said as he slammed a domino onto the table.

"Give me twenty," Brushaud said as he jotted down twenty five points for my father and twenty for himself.

My father spent two days putting everything he took out of his body back into it. Brushaud never bothered him. On the third day, my father was back to normal.

Playing dominoes was a sure sign of that.

To my father, playing dominoes was confession to a Catholic. It was therapeutic. He played dominoes in prison to preserve his sanity. It was the one thing that crossed over perfectly from prison to the real world.

Even after my father came down from his high, he struggled to repair his physical appearance. But his mind always came back sound. He played a game of dominoes as though it was multivariable calculus.

Brushaud did, too.

Brushaud had a flexible work schedule. He normally worked weekday mornings and he spent afternoons with my father. Brushaud got my father caught up on all the good movies he missed while he was locked up. And he introduced my father to HBO's "The Wire".

My father loved it. It only took him two weeks to watch all five seasons. I thought it was odd. "The Wire" was all about drugs – selling it and using it. I didn't get how someone addicted to crack could watch a show about it. I thought it would either embarrass the person or tempt them.

It didn't do either one to my father.

My father also became my brother's in-house chef. He cooked everything from barbeque ribs to smothered pork chops to prison pancakes. Prison pancakes were pancakes covered in peanut butter and topped with maple syrup. It was the kind of concoction that would give someone sugar diabetes after the first bite.

The main thing my father did at Brushaud's house was clean. My grandma cleaned rich people's homes for a living, so she knew a thing or two about cleanliness. She passed that to my father. He kept everything disinfected.

Three weeks into my father's stay, Brushaud got comfortable.

Things were cool. My brother ate my father's version of gourmet cuisine every day and always had a movie and domino buddy. He was partially holding my father hostage.

Brushaud didn't want my father to leave.

My father never used drugs and never caused any problems while at my brother's. He liked it there. Contrary to my grandma's house, it was cozy. Brushaud kept the apartment dark and cold. My grandma's house was vibrant. And she didn't believe in excessively running the air conditioner.

I stopped by before work on my off days. No matter what time I stopped by, my father was always up to play dominoes or to cook whatever I wanted.

But we knew he couldn't stay forever.

Thanks to weeks of soaking his body in Epsom Salt and Clorox Bleach, my father's body was healing. The scares in his legs turned to scabs. The swelling and blisters in his feet were gone, and he was able to walk again.

* * *

"I'm ready," my father told Brushaud.

It was December first – the morning of Brushaud's twenty-ninth birthday. My father had been rehabbing and hiding out at Brushaud's for a little more than a month.

It was time.

"You wanna go anywhere before you turn yourself in?" Brushaud asked.

"Yea, let's go get some Mexican food."

* * *

"You sure this is what you want to do?" Brushaud asked as he and my father sat in the parking lot of the county jail.

My father nodded.

When they walked into the building, my brother told the police officers that my father was there to turn himself in. They looked surprised. They didn't even bother handcuffing him.

"Just have a seat so we can get you processed," an officer told my father.

Brushaud left after the officers started the processing phase. He sat out in his car for fifteen minutes just to make sure my father didn't have a change of heart.

Then he went home.

Brushaud and my father's PO were in constant contact. His PO couldn't say for sure what would happen to my father. My father's fate was in the hands of a parole board, which consisted of my father's PO and several other people.

His PO told my brother that if both my brother and I appeared at the hearing, it could help my father's chances of being released.

* * *

"I know my father broke the law," I told the parole board. "But my father has a drug addiction. He has gone to prison so many times and each time he's come back with that same addiction. Prison can't help him. We can. My brother and I both live here. We have jobs and are prepared to support him in every way."

I fought back tears as my father sat across the glass room in an orange jumpsuit and handcuffs.

As I exited the room, Brushaud entered.

He told the parole board that my father could live with him and that he would make sure my father sought rehab. After that, we left. I went to work, and Brushaud went home.

My father spent two months in prison before he was released on house arrest. He was given an ankle monitor and told to stay at my grandma's house. He couldn't leave the house without his PO's consent. And even then, he had to leave and return at a certain time. He was supposed to wear the ankle monitor for sixty days.

He almost made it.

TRACK 14

My grandma is one of the scariest people I've ever known. Growing up, her house was the last place I wanted to be if it was ever raining outside. Even if she heard a little thunder, she turned off all the lights and any other electrical appliances. It didn't matter if lotto numbers were being drawn or if there was three seconds left in an NBA Finals game, my grandma did not play. She would rather sit in her house staring at the walls and fanning herself with a paper towel to keep cool before she let lightning strike her house. There is only one other thing my grandma fears more than she does lightning: driving at night.

I've never seen her do it.

Only my father has.

* * *

It was late. The only lights outside were street lights and cigarette lighters. My grandma stuffed a metal chain in her purse and got into the driver's seat of her gray 1986 Monte Carlo.

"If you see Bruce, don't sell him nothing," my grandma yelled out to people as she rode through the

Wheatley Courts, stopping at every breezeway to make sure she was heard.

People might have pretended, but no one would've really listened to her.

For one, the drug game wasn't personal; it was a business. I'd seen mother and son working the same corner. I'd even seen a dude sell to his own family. And two, nobody on the streets knew who Bruce was.

They knew Anthony Montgomery, Tony for short. My father didn't trust anybody, especially other addicts. He always feared that people would turn on him. Crack cocaine only magnified that fear. He was afraid someone would drop his name to the cops or to a family member that was looking for him.

Occasionally, someone from his past – an old high school buddy or someone like that –saw him on the streets.

"Hey Bruce," they'd say.

"Naw man... I don't go by Bruce out here. I'm Tony."

And that's what everybody knew him as.

My father didn't have a middle name. He was just Bruce Callis. But he said if he did have a middle name he would've wanted it to be Anthony. That's where the street name came from. He said the last name Montgomery just flowed well.

* * *

"Say man, some ole lady riding around looking for somebody named Bruce," a guy told my father. "She's telling everybody not to sell to him."

My father knew it was my grandma.

As he looked down from the upstairs apartment

he was in, he saw my grandma's head poking out the window of her old Cutlass. My father sat in the apartment watching as my grandma pleaded with random strangers. He hid out until my grandma left.

After that, it was back to the hustle.

* * *

My father stayed on the streets three days at a time. The other four days of the week were spent recovering. In the seventy-two hours he spent away from home, forty-two of those hours were devoted to smoking crack. The other thirty were reserved for hustling the money and scoring crack.

There was an art to his hustle.

The downtown area was like an all-you-can-eat buffet for con artists. Downtown had something most other parts of town didn't have – tourists. In other words, downtown was filled with people dumb enough to give their money away. Money was always good when there was an annual convention in town. Convention goers were the easiest people to con.

My father knew that.

Whether selling something door-to-door or at a store, every hustle requires presentation. My father always wore clean, white sneakers. Clean, white sneakers gave the impression that he wasn't a drifter. Above the shoes, he wore ironed blue jeans and a pull-over Polo shirt. Blue jeans gave him a comfortable, approachable appearance.

The Polo shirt gave him sophistication.

White people liked that look.

My father never hustled in a T-shirt. T-shirts didn't

bring in good money. He kept a clean face and a bald head. He always carried a map of the city with him. He wanted people to believe that he was a tourist. The map trick always worked. He walked through downtown asking people in passing if they were familiar with the downtown area.

If they said yes, he left them alone.

He didn't fool with local people.

No matter how much he craved for crack, my father never begged people for money. Beggars only got a dollar here and there. My father had a rule: If he wasn't making at least twenty dollars an hour, then he didn't need to be out there. Once he found the right person, he went to work.

"This has been the worse day of my life."

That's how he started each encounter.

He followed that sentence with different scenarios. Sometimes he was in the military, other times he was just like them – a tourist. But instead of talking directly to them and giving them a sad story, he talked to himself. He would chew himself out, saying things like "I'm so stupid and I can't believe I let such and such do this."

The trick was to put a person's disbelief in suspension without over talking. As soon as a person gave him feedback, he knew he had them. He gave people his house keys, his wallet and anything else that would help assure them that he was a good guy. He didn't care about any of that stuff.

He needed money.

After he hustled up enough money, which was

normally four hundred or so dollars, he had to score the crack. The dope game was a tricky business. Dealers wanted customers to be loyal. Addicts just wanted to get high. Some dope men robbed and beat addicts if they saw them buying from someone else. It was crazy, kind of like a local grocery chain robbing and beating you because they caught you shopping at Wal-Mart.

My father was like most addicts – he wanted to get high. But he also wanted respect from dope dealers. He didn't give his business to just anybody. He liked dealers that were laid back, and not aggressive. He preferred to work with older guys. He hated youngsters. They were like a box of chocolate; he never knew what to expect. But sometimes, he had to work with the youngsters.

No matter who my father worked with, he liked to get high at crack houses in the Denver Heights and Wheatley Courts. At both project housing complexes there was an underlined rule: fry it where you buy it. That meant my father could score and get high at the same place. Both projects also housed the freakiest and nastiest girls. My father enjoyed getting high and then having sex in a hallway or back room of a crack house with random women.

Crack was an aphrodisiac for him.

It seemed crazy to believe that crack could have that kind of effect on people. Crack was just a small, white rock. The high was over before it started. It didn't have a loud smell. Crack had a dull odor, like somebody had just blown out a candle.

But it was enough.

My father raved about his crack-house experiences

as though they were backyard barbeques. I pictured people sitting around smoking crack and laughing over a game of dominoes.

It was nothing like that.

There was no music. No games. No talking. No water, no lights. With the exception of a few chairs, crack houses were empty. The houses looked as though people were moving out. If you weren't smoking, you were having sex.

That's it.

Of course there were the side effects – frequent bowel movements, loss of appetite and sleepless days and nights. Sometimes, the side effects were worse. It normally took my father twenty-five to thirty-five hits before he felt good. One time, after that twenty-fifth or so hit, my father started seeing stuff. He saw a roach about two feet away from him. And then the roach disappeared. My father thought the roach was on him, so he walked to the store to buy roach spray.

He felt the roach on his leg, so he sprayed the area with the roach spray. But the more he sprayed, the more my father felt the roach crawling on different parts of his body. He sprayed his entire body – including his underwear, socks and shoes – in an attempt to kill a roach that never existed.

"Man, it smells like roach spray in here," a man standing next to my father said.

"Oh, yea... I just killed a roach in the corner over there," my father replied.

But it was all worth it to my father.

Getting high was fun.

He wasn't just addicted to crack; he was addicted to the hustle.

After a few days of endless crack highs, chips and soda and no sleep, my father could barely walk or talk. When he got to that point, where he could fall asleep walking, then it was time to go home.

Going home was the hard part.

Most times my father caught the bus or walked home. His feet felt like they were on fire. His feet were so swollen that he couldn't put on or take off his shoes. He smelled awful. He had constant arthritis pains in his fingers from flicking a lighter so many times. He had muscle spasms in his wrists from holding a pipe for so many hours. But somehow, he always made it home.

My grandma wouldn't dare give him a key.

Instead, she told him that if he knocked she would always let him in. My grandma hated my father's addiction. She rarely slept when he was on the streets. Sometimes she would threaten to leave my dad out on the streets. But no matter what time of day or night, he staggered in.

And she kept her promise.

My father never said a word when he got in the house. Sure, the shame was on his face, but we never could tell if it was sincere or not. He just went straight to the bathroom. He'd stay in there for at least an hour trying to wash away seventy-two hours of filth. Then he'd make his way to the kitchen to satisfy his massive appetite. He ate everything from pancakes topped with cake icing, peanut butter and syrup to fried chicken with all the fixings.

He ate until he fell asleep.

He slept for what seemed like days at a time. Even when he was awake, his speech was distorted and his eyes went back and forth in his head. He rocked and scratched himself in his sleep. After a day or two of that same routine, he was fine.

"I went out there looking for you, Bruce," my grandma said.

My father sat at the table in silence.

TRACK 15

They looked just alike.

Isaac, as the congregation called him, was said to have been six-feet-three-inches tall with his shoes off. His skin was a dark coat of brown. He wore a thick mustache and a short afro.

No smile.

There was nothing distinct about anything else on his face except for his nose.

His nose told it all.

My father had a nose just like that. I didn't know much about Isaac. In fact, before today, I didn't even know his name was Isaac. I thought his name was Jack. I didn't know what year he was born or how old he was. The program didn't disclose that information either, which seemed odd. But then again, there was a lot of information left off that program. It didn't even mention my father as a survivor.

I hated funerals, especially the kind when everyone stood at a podium pretending the deceased person was the closest thing to Jesus we'd ever seen.

"I'm going up there," my brother Boshavar joked.

"Yea, right," I said.

Boshavar was a hot head when it came to situations like this. He was always the first out of his seat and the last to bite his tongue. But I knew he wasn't going to get up there and say anything. And even if he tried, he was sandwiched between me, Brushaud and my dad.

One of us would've stopped him.

I had never been to a funeral with my father before. He looked nice. He weighed a lot more than he usually did, but the brown dress shirt and pants hid it well. Brushaud wore a blue dress shirt with a red tie and black slacks. And Boshavar wore all black.

So did I.

It was hard to gage what kind of man Isaac was. Those who spoke of him at the service said he was a Christian man, a great father, and so on. But before the funeral, I'd never heard anyone speak of him that way.

"Nette, if anybody should go up there, it should be you," my father whispered.

"Me?"

Did my father come to the funeral high? I barely knew Jack or Isaac or whatever his name was. I wasted several years, two Father's Day holidays, and one Hallmark card trying to meet the man that was said to have been my dad's biological father.

* * *

"What do you want?" Jack screamed at me as I approached the entrance of his front door. "I'm sick."

I ran back to my car, and vowed to never go back again.

The only image I had of Jack was a black, ugly

man. He looked like death. He sat near his front door in a wheelchair. Both his legs had been amputated. He was shriveled up and frail. He didn't look anything like the picture on the front of the funeral program. Most people don't. My father knew that story. But he'd suffered far more than that little encounter.

After all, Isaac was his father.

"Go, Nette."

I didn't want to go up there. But I knew I had to. When my father looked at me, it was as though he was a kid again. I saw hurt in his eyes and for the first time, I saw his heart on his sleeve. He couldn't muster up enough courage to go up there. He knew I was strong enough to do it on his behalf. He could've asked Brushaud or Boshavar, but he didn't.

So I got up, took a deep breathe, made sure my panties weren't showing, and walked to the side of the church to wait for my turn to speak. Both Brushaud and Boshavar came with me. As we waited, they kept asking me what I was going to say.

"I got this," I assured them.

But I didn't know what I was going to say. I wanted to tell everyone that all I knew about Isaac was that he loved to drink and didn't love us. I wanted everyone to know that he was nothing more than an alcoholic who had abandoned my father as a young child.

It was his fault my father was on drugs.

My father always warned me about drinking and drugs. He advised me to never become addicted to anything. He said addictions ran in our blood. For years, I never knew what he meant until I found out his father was an alcoholic. My father told me Jack was always drunk.

He wasn't a social drinker, but more of a loner instead.

He used to ride down country roads with one bottle of gin in his hand and another one tucked under his seat. He used to get into car accidents all the time, but laws against driving while intoxicated came later. The cops would just pull him over and let him sleep the alcohol off.

It was hard to believe that the same drunkard who rode down those country roads was the same man the preacher was glorifying. What was even harder to believe was that I was going to chime in with a little glorification of my own.

I guess it made sense for me to speak and not my brothers. I didn't know much about Jack, but even so, I knew more than they did. My brothers never seemed bothered by Jack's absence.

I was the one who wanted to know him. I didn't think it was fair that I was robbed of a father and a grandfather. The more I sought information about Jack, the more I learned about my father.

"You want me to say something," Brushaud asked me.

"I told you, I got this."

I called on God for a quick favor.

I needed something short and sweet to say. My true feelings didn't matter. He was dead anyway. No one there deserved to know what he'd done. God knew. When we got to the podium, I wasn't sure if it was polite to smile, considering the occasion.

I smiled anyway.

I was brief.

I introduced me and my brothers and mentioned that we were his grandchildren from his first son. I mentioned that we never got a chance to know him, but were pleased to hear that he was a wonderful man. And then we sat down. The few people at the funeral who knew us, said my short talk was classy. I felt like it was nothing but lies, aside from the part about who we were.

But my father gave me that nod of assurance.

He was proud of me.

I never saw that proud look often, but I imagined it was the kind of look a father gave a child after hitting a game-winning shot. As we walked back to the pew where my father was seated, I could feel the congregation's eyes all over me. And after the service ended, we got our fifteen minutes of fame. People, old and young, swarmed around us like we were honey to their beehives.

Everyone wanted an explanation.

"Who are you?" some light-skinned lady with a crooked gold tooth asked my dad.

"Jack was my father," my dad said, with an odd sense of pride.

"I'm a Luckey," said one older man, with a bushy mustache and few teeth. After each word he said, cigarette smoke blew out from the holes where his teeth used to be. "And I didn't find out until I was thirty-six-years-old."

Jack's mother's maiden name was Luckey. She had been dead for quite some time. But my father said she owned a soul food restaurant.

"I guess we kinfolk," the older man said as he reached out to shake my father's hand. "And don't feel bad man, Jack was my cousin, and I hadn't seen him in twenty years. Nobody had," the older man added.

I don't know if it was the one-hundred-degree weather that July brought San Antonio every year or the cigarette smoke the old man kept blowing in my face, but it was hotter than four fat women piled together in the back of an old Cadillac with no air conditioner. So we posed for a few pictures, said our goodbyes, and left.

"When was the last time you talked to Jack, Daddy?" Boshavar asked on the car ride from the funeral.

"I know the answer," I butted in. "The last time daddy talked to Jack was when he was going to the prom."

"Yep, Nette probably knows the story better than me," my dad said.

"How do you know?" Boshavar asked.

"Mama told me the other day. She said she was with Daddy when he went to pick up the prom shoes from Jack."

"Yea, see... I needed some shoes for prom," my father started out. "And I wanted this one pair, but they were sixty-five dollars. So I asked my daddy to buy them for me and he did."

It seemed like a sweet story. Boshavar seemed touched. And even though I knew more of the story,

I wouldn't dare say it to my father's face. My mother told me a story very similar to that. But instead of it being a heartfelt gift exchange between father and son, it was more of a 'take this shit and let me get back to this bottle' exchange. Jack was drunk, and my mother said she remembered every word he said.

"Now boy, take these shoes. And that's a pretty girl, so you better treat her right," my mother remembers him saying, in a slurred drunken voice.

My mother even said Jack and my dad spoke one or two times after that. But it was much of the same. Jack was drunk most of the time and didn't have a care or worry about my father.

"But you know, it's hard to be mad at him now because I know I wasn't there for y'all," my dad said.

He was right and wrong.

He wasn't there for us.

But he had every right to be mad at Jack. Jack didn't put the crack pipe to his mouth, but he sure as hell wasn't there to knock it out of his hand either. My dad never shared too much about Jack. He only said that as a kid he questioned and wondered if Jack was his real father.

There wasn't any DNA testing back then, but if you saw a picture of Jack and a picture of my father, their resemblance would put a DNA test to shame. Early on, no one could blame my father for having his doubts. My grandma and Jack were never married. He and my grandma were just boyfriend and girlfriend and not for very long. She had six children. The other five were all by one man. His last name was Callis, which is also my dad's last name.

I don't know why my grandma didn't give my dad Jack's last name. Maybe she wanted all of her children to have the same last name. I don't know. And as I've gotten older, I've learned there are some questions you just don't ask. In his heart, my dad said he knew Jack was his father. But there were times when he wished he wasn't.

When my dad was real little, he and Jack had a pretty good relationship. Jack used to pick him up every Saturday afternoon. His breath always stunk of liquor, but my dad didn't care.

He just wanted a father.

And for the most part, as long as my grandma and Jack were still messing around, he had one. But after the thrill was gone, so was Jack's relationship with my father.

He used to promise to pick my dad up at the same place, same time. And every Saturday for years, my dad sat on the steps right outside his family's three-bedroom duplex waiting for Jack. From those steps, my father watched as cars entered and exited the highway. But none of them were ever Jack. And even though Jack didn't come the week before, my father always believed he would be there the next week. He sat on those steps from sun up to sun down, refusing to even go to the bathroom to pee.

"If I go somewhere then I might miss him," my father used to tell my grandma. "And he might think I wasn't out here waiting for him."

As the street lights flickered on, my grandma would

have to drag my father into the house. He was always in tears by the day's end.

"Come on in, baby. He ain't coming. He done lied again."

Around my dad's eighteenth birthday, he stopped letting Jack be the barrier of broken promises. He stopped calling Jack. And he only sat on the steps outside his house to roll and smoke joints. My father grew up around two men: Jack, who had abandoned him most of his life and his stepdad, who was just as bad. My father's stepdad, who was the father of my dad's five siblings, was a drunk too.

My dad was young, but he still remembers watching my grandma and his stepdad fight. They fought so often that my grandma slept with a switch blade under her pillow. My grandma did the best she could raising six children, but she couldn't teach my dad how to be a man or a father.

He taught himself.

"But you're still alive, Daddy. So it's not too late for our relationship," I said as we got out the car and walked into this expensive Mexican restaurant off of Broadway.

I was normally a picky eater, but since it was right after Jack's funeral, I let my dad choose where we ate. He always chose Mexican food. As long as it was Mexican, it didn't matter to him if the food came from a gourmet kitchen or a hole in the wall. Brushaud was the sadity one. Both he and my dad had an obsession with Mexican food.

The only difference was Brushaud had to have the

best of the best. This restaurant was his home away from home. The nachos, fajitas, and margaritas were all good, but overpriced. My tab – a lunch order of quesadillas, nachos and two strawberry margaritas – was close to fifty dollars. But I got over it. I was just glad to see us altogether. I was even more pleased to see my father a little overweight. His weight was always an indication of how he was doing. If he was thin, he wasn't too many days removed from the streets and vice versa.

"Yea, Nette, you're right. It's just been hard sometimes for me as a father because I never had anyone show me how to be one."

I understood that.

TRACK 16

"Who is that?" my father asked as he turned up the volume on my car stereo and bobbed his head back and forth.

"That's Lil' Wayne," I said.

"Man, Nette, I like that."

As I drove past the Wheatley Courts in fear, my father was in the passenger's seat cool, calm and collected, listening to rap music like it was the audio version of the Bible. I was trying to gather myself. I could still hear the sirens but when I looked in my rearview mirror, the cops were gone.

Even though we didn't get caught, maybe I needed that fear. That fear kept me grounded. It reminded that even though my father was the parent, he still needed me to step in and parent sometimes. Parenting my father wasn't always about right and wrong. That day, I felt like a parent who had to choose between life and death for her son.

I chose life.

He was struggling. And even though it hurt me and damn near criminalized me, it was worth it. My father always said that even as young as three years old, I was like a little mother to him. I was just a kid then, but something always tugged at my heart when I was around my father.

"How did you get home Daddy?" I used to ask my father as he stumbled through our apartment door. "Did you take the bus? Did you walk? Did a friend give you a ride home?"

After a broken smile, my father would hurry past me and into the bathroom to shower and shave. Most nights, I fell asleep by the door as I waited for my father to come out. It didn't matter if it was helping him onto the couch, taking off his shoes or pouring him a glass of Kool-Aid, I felt like my father needed me.

A few months had passed since that weed-run. Things hadn't changed much, but they were getting better. My father was still smoking weed, but crack was looking like a distant memory. He had been out of prison for three years now, which was the longest he'd been out since I was a baby.

And for the first time in years, there was a woman in his life. My father did his best to downplay the situation. But I knew he liked Pooh. They had this "Me and Mrs. Jones" kind of relationship. Because of that, he was afraid to get seriously involved with Pooh. She had just as much baggage as he did. Their friendship dated back to my father's days in the Sutton Homes when he rolled with his childhood best friends, Billy and Chris.

Chris dated Pooh.

But back then, Chris was a womanizer – the kind

of guy that treated women like objects. Pooh was just a pawn to his chess game. Or so he said. But that was a long time ago. Pooh had been married and divorced since then. And Chris was married now. Chris and my father were still friends, but they lived in different states and lived very different lives. I wasn't sure what Chris did, but whenever I talked to him, he bragged about Sunday golf outings and out-of-town business trips. He described Pooh to me as a girl that used to like him. And if that was true, then my father had every right to hang out with her.

But there was more.

Pooh had a man. I don't know if she had a thing for drug addicts, but her boyfriend was addicted to crack, too. My father told me that Pooh's boyfriend was more hooked on dope than he was. Her boyfriend had a stroke two weeks before she and my father reconnected. He was in the hospital, and she wasn't sure how long it would take him to recover. If he made a full recovery, then the chances of my father and Pooh working out were slim to none. In a sense, my father was banking everything on her boyfriend's suffering.

So was I.

Even though Pooh had baggage, she was good for my father. She had her own place on the Northeast side of San Antonio, which was at least an hour or two walk from my father's usual hangouts. A few days a week, she worked at a vehicle assembly plant.

And best of all, she was regular.

Now what I mean by regular is that she looked like a normal person – not some skanky-looking white girl or the female version of Notorious B.I.G. Pooh was about the same color as me; a dark coat of caramel. But she was mixed with Mexican and black. Her hair was long and straight in its natural form.

She was a beer drinker. And sometimes she overdid it. But my father and Pooh made sense. About a month into their relationship, my father called me to get some birthday celebration ideas. It was Pooh's birthday. He wanted to take her to a buffet; somewhere like Golden Corral.

"Nette, what's wrong with taking her to Golden Corral?"

"Daddy, are you serious?" I asked. "No woman wants to go to a buffet for her birthday. Take her somewhere nice."

"I'm not trying to spend a lot of money, Nette."

That was my father.

He didn't believe in spending a lot of money on food and stuff like that. He was content with fast food and cheap Mexican restaurants. But Brushaud and I convinced him to take her to this one restaurant on the North Side – the good side of town. This restaurant had good food and even better drink specials. It wasn't too pricey; sort of like an upscale Chili's.

But Pooh loved it.

* * *

My father slept at Pooh's house more nights than he did at my grandma's. Even though he was playing house with her, he still stood on the notion that nothing was going on between them. But I knew better. I also knew that it would take one hell of a woman to show up and somehow completely transform my father from a three-day high, four days clean routine to a laidback, always-at-home guy.

That's what Pooh did. My father had been clean for three months. When he and I talked on the phone, it was different. There was a spark of joy in his voice. Every time we talked, he was with Pooh.

His initial worries of Chris and Pooh's boyfriend were meaningless now. I knew that rumors and gossip had a way of traveling, so I was sure Chris knew about Pooh and my father. And Pooh's boyfriend was more of a speed bump than a detour sign. He recovered from the stroke, but he moved in with his mother after his hospital release.

One night, Pooh's boyfriend's mother called to see if he could come stay the night with Pooh. Pooh told his mother that she wasn't home and didn't know what time she would be. I guess Pooh was so drunk that night that she never realized her boyfriend's mother called Pooh on Pooh's house phone.

Their relationship ended that night. And Pooh's relationship with my father intensified. My father let his guard down. But the more he spent time with her, the more he searched for flaws. He told me that Pooh was a good friend, but that I didn't know everything he knew about her. He was right. I didn't know much about her.

I knew she couldn't handle her liquor, but that was all I knew. My father hated that about her. Liquor made her morph into an alter ego. She talked and socialized more when she had a beer in her hand. My father wasn't social around people he didn't know or trust.

And he didn't trust Pooh's neighbors.

After two or three beers, Pooh let loose. Just as always, she transformed into the life of her neighborhood. People she barely knew passed by to drink and party at her house. One of her neighbors sold weed. He was a young dude, in his twenties. My father bought weed from him a few times. He hated getting weed from Pooh's neighbor, but Pooh's neighbor was the closest weed dealer my father knew.

"Say man, I'm selling this for twenty dollars," the weed man told my father.

"I'm good," my father replied.

"Come on man, this shit is good."

"If he don't buy it, I will," Pooh butted in, before my father could respond.

"Did you hear me tell him that I didn't want it?" my father asked. "And you don't even smoke weed, so I don't know why you're even in this conversation."

My father hated people all in his business. And he never liked the way Pooh was when she was drunk. I can't say for certain what happened after he told her that. But as far as I know, it got ugly. The neighbors left and so did my father. I finally got in touch with my father about three or four days later. He was at my grandma's house. My grandma said he had just walked through the door.

"You haven't been calling me... where you been at Daddy?" I asked.

"What... when's the last time we talked?"

"Monday... and today is Thursday."

"Oh... you right, Nette... I ain't been doing nothing... just stayed the night at this Mexican girl's house last night."

My father never lied to me, but sometimes he talked in parables. He and I both knew what he meant. He always coded crack as though it was a white or Mexican girl. I sometimes wondered why crack couldn't be a black woman. But it never failed, if my father said he spent the night with a woman of another race then it meant he spent the night getting high.

"Did you mess up last night?" I asked.

"Yes, I did," he said. "I used crack cocaine last night."

"What happened?"

He said he never put his hands on Pooh, but he talked to her real bad. After that, he left her house. He didn't know what to do.

"I was so mad, man," he said. "I hated the feeling I was feeling and I wanted to change it. Crack don't make me feel good, but I knew it would make me feel different. I just didn't know what to do with my emotions."

Crazy thing is – I understood what he meant. As I listened to him tell me how he felt, I finally began to understand it. Three years ago, as I sat in my car writing that rap, I was him. I was looking for anything to take me away. I wanted to get high.

As he spoke I thought about my whole life. I started using boys to fill the hole my father left. And then I needed more. Music was that more. It made me feel different. I even used music as a kid when I went by the name Lady T. Back then I wrote lyrics to make me feel like I was a "somebody" because on the inside I felt like a "nobody". I used music to make me feel better about love and a lack thereof as an adolescent. I even used music to help me black out after I took my father to buy weed. My father and I were no different. We were doing the same thing. I was just doing it legally. On the outside, crack seemed so much more destructive than music. But internally, music was just as damaging.

Crack cocaine was my father's drug. Music was mine.

It made sense. Music has always been a universal language for the broken. Broken hearts. Broken homes. Broken promises.

So has crack.

Neither of the two was potent enough to erase your past or change your present circumstances, but they could alter your state of mind. And that was enough, even if it was only momentarily.

We turned to drugs for much of the same reasons. Initially, it was that hint of temptation and curiosity. Every time I listened to music, I felt chills in my body. I wanted more of that and less of the pain. My father wanted those same chills, but not from music.

We both got what we were looking for.

Our reasons transformed from flirtatious experiments to hiding places. My father was running from the skeletons in his closet. He snorted, shot up and smoked anything he could to dodge adult-like problems. My father was emotionally incompetent. Every time things got tough, crack cocaine called and he ran.

I was running, too.

I didn't know it then, but the night I broke down in my car, I was running from my father. I was still that three-year-old little girl standing at the front door, wondering where my father was.

My father was still that broken little boy trying to be better than his alcoholic father. He was that youngest child of six left wondering why he had to be the sibling with a different father. He was that adolescent boy who never wanted to live to be an adult because he'd seen too much pain as a kid.

Of all things, he was human.

He was my father. And he was guilty of what I'd been guilty of all my life; letting my emotions get the best of me. As I sat on the other end of the phone listening to my father tell me the reason he went back to crack after three months, my heart cried for us both. It took me being "the other woman" for me to understand my father's obsession with "the other woman."

It was emotions.

And so, as I searched for words to encourage him, I thought back to what he always told me, "I before E,' Daddy... intellect before emotion."

To Bootie
My Brother & True Close Friend
Thanks for the Love & Support
You've Shown me over the Years
Much Love
Bruce

CPSIA information can be obtained at www.ICGtesting.com
Printed in the USA
LVOW060222100113

315125LV00001B/2/P